Aging: An Album of People Growing Old

Aging:
An Album of
People Growing Old

Shura Saul

John Wiley & Sons, Inc., New York • London • Sydney • Toronto

B + N 5,50 | 12 | 13 | 78 (2 copies)

Library of Congress Cataloging in Publication Data:
Saul, Shura.
 Aging: an album of people growing old.

 Originally issued as part of the author's thesis, Columbia University.
 Bibliography: p.
 1. Aged—United States. 2. Education of the aged. 3. Old age assistance—United States. I. Title.
[DNLM: 1. Aging. WT104 S256a 1974]
HQ1064.U5S28 301.43′5 73-21973
ISBN 0-471-75505-2
ISBN 0-471-75506-0 (pbk.)

Printed in the United States of America

10-9 8 7 6 5

To my parents and the elders of my family
—my challenging and inspiring role models

To all the older people with whom I have worked
—my many teachers

To my children
—you will also grow old

Preface

I have written this book because I believe it will help people to learn about aging in modern times. As such, it is concerned with two processes—learning and aging. The stories, all of which are true, have happened during my 20 years of professional experience with old people and with many students in a variety of educational programs. This *Album* is part of my doctoral dissertation which may be found in the library of Teachers College, Columbia University.

I feel deeply that improving our understanding of senescence (the latter period of life during which we grow old) will enhance our understanding of life. Therefore, I have written this book for teachers and students who expect to work with people in any field of human relationships and services. Every worker in these fields may someday expect to come into contact with an older person and his family. I have found, in my own teaching, that students respond to and learn from anecdotal material taken from experience, their own as well as the experience of others. Retelling stories helps to bring to life the realities of social and individual concerns and discloses new dimensions of situations. Incidents that might appear meaningless at first glance become significant when a more insightful view is taken. The vignettes in this *Album* are offered as springboards to a second look at life, at people, and at the helping process.

The use of this book as a means for learning stems from the view that:

Education for service must include understanding of the emotional component in giving, receiving, and using help.
Awareness of one's own feelings is primary to understanding those of other people.
Literature and the arts are significant educational media through which this awareness can be developed and heightened.

The potential helping agent will sharpen his sensitivity to others through learning experiences with art media.

The development of this *Album* was a unique process. In addition to my own vignettes, I gathered contributions from many young and old people. A total of about 40 pieces was submitted (with no indication of their authorship) to a panel of 54 reader-judges consisting of students, professionals, and elderly people.

The student-readers, numbering 18, were members of graduate and undergraduate programs in a variety of disciplines including education, social work, psychology, sociology, nursing, medicine, and law.

The elderly readers (there were 16 of them) were all over 70 years of age. Of these, 6 were active in community and mental health programs, 5 live in institutions for the aged (both homes and nursing homes), and 5 others are living at home and functioning in the community at large. Several of these older people are professionals and 3 of them were still working.

The 20 professional readers represented a wide range of helping professions. They included administrators of programs (both for aging and for community-at-large), educators, psychiatrists, psychologists, pharmacists, nurses, social workers, and medical doctors as well as artists, art therapists, and one director of a volunteer program.

All of the readers were asked to respond to the vignettes in terms of their reality, their emotional appeal, and their possible value for learning about aging. Their responses were thoughtful, critical, and enthusiastic. The selections in this *Album* are based on their recommendations.

This book, then, reflects the views of workers, teachers, and students who are involved with educational needs in the field of aging—and of some older people who are, themselves, experiencing the process.

The *Album* suggests that senescence is best understood within an interdisciplinary framework; that there must be recognition of all life factors within an individual situation; that aging is not an illness but a phase of life; and that each of us expects someday to grow old. The book is organized in three major sections.

Part I, "Picture Frames," offers a philosophic viewpoint for considering the circumstances and emotions depicted in the vignettes. In general, the view is humanistic and optimistic—offering a sense of perspective and hope to young and old. The references, culled from the rich and continually growing literature in the field, are intended to encourage further reading and independent study. Teachers will find this section, as well as Part III, useful for developing curricula and topics for class sessions.

Part II, "An Album", should be used creatively by teachers and students. The stories are grouped freely and may be read in any order. The different literary forms of short story, poetry, journalistic accounts, and conversations appeal to different readers.

Of special interest in this section are the contributions of the younger and the older people who shared their ideas and feelings in their own words. The emphasis in these two sections is not on literary expertise, but on communication—the expression of people's emotions and ideas in their own words.

Part III, "Background Discussions," suggests some implications for service and education. Service is viewed within an interdisciplinary context, and education is viewed as combining emotional and cognitive elements. This section also suggests ways of using the material in classes and educational programs.

Like any anthology, this one cannot presume to describe all the shades in the endless spectrum of its concerns. Instead, it suggests a panoramic overview by offering some revealing highlights. A few obvious limitations must be specified here. The people presented in the stories are essentially urban, and they tend to come from lower-middle and working classes. Some of the special circumstances of ethnic minority groups (for example Black, Puerto Rican, and Chicano), who are important in the contemporary American city scene, have not been singled out. The elderly members of these groups have been described as living under conditions of "double jeopardy," combining consequences of discrimination as well as of aging. Sociological literature has shown that these groups, in comparison with others, endure more unemployment, lower income, greater ratios of admission to mental hospitals, a shorter life span, more severe patterns of family disorganization, and the like. In general, these groups are described as living under an exacerbation of conditions faced by all poor older people in the United States. To that extent, some of their concerns are represented here. To have attempted to plumb the quality of their unique problems through only one or two stories would have been inadequate, since they warrant a distinct album of their own.

These are some limitations of this *Album*. If this book is used projectively despite these limitations, readers can begin to examine their own experiences, can develop their own material, and can extend the horizons of their own learning.

Gerontologists have identified a gap between the considerable amount of information available in the field of aging and its usefulness to practice and service. If this book is used as one bridge between theory and practice through the integration of cognitive learning and emotional growth, it will have fulfilled its purpose.

* * *

Since no person lives or works alone, this book involved the support and help of many people.

The students and older people who contributed their writings added vitality and validity to these pictures of aging. The reader-judges helped to make the most valuable selections.

Drs. Leland B. Jacobs and Hope Leichter of Teachers College, Columbia University, provided guidance of a doubly rich nature. From them, I have gained substantive knowledge and an understanding of new ways to learn— and, hence, to teach.

A housewife-mother-teacher could not also be a student and writer without family support. My daughter, my sons and their wives, my parents— all listened, read, contributed, criticized, and encouraged helpfully and appropriately.

My husband, Dr. Sidney Saul, never permitted me to feel that I was working alone and helped me to continue to believe that this book would really be completed.

Jane Ruhl, Jennifer Saul, Philip Millstein, and Arthur Burg were important in the various phases of typing and manuscript reproduction.

To all these helpful friends, there are no adequate words of thanks. I can only hope that now, with the *Album* a reality, they will feel that their efforts are well directed.

Shura Saul

Contents

Aging: An Album of People Growing Old

Part I
Picture Frames

Viewing Aging and
Learning in Our Times

This "album" is a book of snapshots of some real older people. Every individual has been known to the author and every incident has really occurred. These vignettes are presented as highlights of a spectrum of circumstances that may be faced by any aging person in modern times. They are about people growing older in a world unprepared for them. Like all snapshots, they portray only a slice of life.

These men and women are members of a generation born just before, or early in the twentieth century. Their lives span the period of major social change from early industrialism to modern technology. They have contributed their labor, their skills, and their ideas through participation in processes that have revolutionized modern life: from horse-drawn vehicles to jet planes, from gas and kerosene fuel to electricity, and from water mills to nuclear power. Many, uprooted from their homes in other lands, came to this country to start a new life. They have endured and participated in several major wars, more than one severe depression, urbanization and exurbanization—and they have lived to see a few of their grandchildren walk on the moon!

Reared at a time when the skills of elders were relevant to youth, they now find themselves in an era that tends to regard them as "has-beens." However, as a generation, this group, which has pioneered in so many ways, is leading us in yet another—in experiencing the most complex senescence that society has ever known. As they reveal its challenges, they are continuing to perform the significant task of social leadership.

For the first time in the history of man, most people must anticipate a longer life span than ever before. For the first time in the history of our nation, the rate of growth of the "65-plus" population is more rapid than that of the total population.[1] A large and growing aged population is, therefore, a new phenomenon for society.

There are many stereotypes of aging. Whatever their differences, they share one common characteristic. They view the later years of life in one-dimensional terms of "either . . . . or," ranging from "wise, peaceful, and halcyon" to "sterile, passive, dependent, useless, sexless, stagnant." Regardless of its content, any stereotype suggests rigidity, inevitability, and irreversibility. The popular, if amorphous, term "senility" reflects a sense of despair intimating that "there is no use for they are going to die anyway."

The fear of death presses on us all, even in our younger years. Like any fear, it distorts our views, inhibits our creativity, cripples our responses, separates us from each other, and brutalizes our human qualities.

Consequently, many of us turn away from the contemplation of this stage of life, from aged people, and from serving them. The irony lies in the fact that the growing aged population presents an escalating need for all kinds of services, on every level—individual, family, and community. Families are increasingly troubled by the circumstances and problems of aged relatives for which they are unprepared. Many professionals, equally unprepared, fall prey to one of the stereotypes or myths about aging. The Group for Advancement of Psychiatry (GAP) warns that "Age alone frequently leads to stereotyped professional responses."[2]

Most important to realize is that turning away from the aged is a fairly futile stance, since our statistics promise that most of us shall have to face ourselves in the aging process.

These circumstances suggest an ongoing need for a variety of educational programs about the many aspects of growing old, the related social attitudes and their effects on services. GAP observes:

> "One of the attitudes is the stereotype of the older person who must 'inevitably' suffer because of his reduced mobility, health and status. This stereotype is not consistent with the facts which indicate that older people, given the proper supportive circumstances and conditions, are quite capable of enjoying life fully to the end of their lives. It will not do, therefore, to dismiss as inevitable the suffering of old people and to neglect the social responsibility toward them."[3]

Clearly, as the need to understand and serve older people increases, the myths and stereotypes of aging must be dispelled. This is a challenge to educators, as well as to practitioners, who must add the problem of these stereotypes to other concerns of preparing workers for the helping professions. Common educational concerns include developing attitudes of hope and acceptance of social and individual change as well as understanding people and their circumstances. The modern teacher must find and use media through which to counter the effects of contemporary alienation on students, and to affirm common elements of human relationship—commitment, caring, respect. Although these are components of the human personality (as per Maslow, Montague, Rogers, among others), their immutability cannot be taken for granted in the face of the brutalizing thrust of modern industrialism. Teachers in the human services must seek fundamentally human ways of sharing knowledge, experience, and feelings; must dig down through layers of acquisition of mere information to reawaken the essential spirit of human interchange that underlies the service professions. "Renewal of society can go forward," says Gardner, "only if somebody cares."[4]

Caring is the very essence of human service. In the modern era of automated production, depersonalization, and alienation, this tenet requires special emphasis. The giver of service is the provider of help . . . a human being in a chain of human beings who are interdependent on each other for survival. The helping person may not be alienated. The service may not be depersonalized.

This approach to teaching "recognizes and nourishes the humanity of the student"[5] and suggests a basic question, how do we teach feelings?

One answer is that we cannot *teach feelings,* but we can *learn about them.* We can become aware of them and understand how they affect behavior. For such learning, the creative teacher must utilize a wide range of methods and media. The art media lend themselves in exciting ways to heighten awareness and augment understanding.

"A work of art," says Langer, "is an expressive form . . . and what it expresses is human feeling . . . works of art are projections of 'felt life'. . . They are images of feeling that formulate it for our cognition. What is artistically good is whatever is articulate and presents feeling to our understanding."[6]

The learning process involves experience plus interpretation within an emotional climate conducive to growth and change. The use of art forms can be significant aids in comprehending a human state by offering an opportunity to "feel an experience without actually experiencing it," as Professor Leland Jacobs of Columbia has aptly phrased it. Recognizing these links between feeling and cognition highlights the value of teaching through emotional and experiential methods as well as through offering knowledge and developing skills.

Educators are called on to help students find ways of appreciating the alive qualities of human experience; to extend the electric impulses of growth and change to more than a single person within a single experience; to utilize the impact of reality in the educational process. One way is to use the "life story of real people." A chain of life events is presented that, in retelling, reveals a flow and rhythm to occurrences different from what they might have seemed while they were happening. "Case histories" present the facts of these events. "Life stories" add the feeling component—whether it be conceptualized or conveyed through the writers imagery. The full impact of their emotional context are key considerations in the learning process.

There is another value in the threading of real incidents into a story sequence. In practice, the service-giver is usually called on to intervene in a single situation within a life chain. There is often little time, in the giving of the service, to learn much about the recipient as a person. When the service is underpinned by an imaginative view of "the whole person" within his own life continuum, it becomes more graceful, sensitive, appropriate, and meaningful to both giver and receiver. The helping agent, having stored within himself the richness of many "life stories" can draw on this fund of experiences to serve and understand another human being, even in a brief encounter.

Retelling stories of people's needs and some ways of meeting them is a viable teaching method. Offered as examples of what "really happened," it becomes an illustration of what can happen, may happen, and does happen. Significant dimensions of the experience are recalled that may not have been noticed while it was endured. There is learning in both "success" and "failure."

Relating theoretical information to personal knowledge and experience heightens individual awareness and insight. Reading about people offers the opportunity for personal recollection and reevaluation as the reader is reminded of his own stories and experiences with grandparents, aged neighbors, and family friends.

The literary presentation of real stories enhances emotional as well as intellectual understanding, an important component in the education of service workers who must shape attitudes as well as gather knowledge. Greene says, "An authentic literary experience . . . turns a person back into himself, his reality, his spontaneity . . . he must reach deeply into the 'well' of himself and select from his accumulated experiences that which connects with and lends life to, the world created by book."[7] Empathic identification and relationships can be fostered through such self-awareness.

The view is widened. Horizons expand. The stereotype may then fade, and be replaced with a less frightening and more realistic picture. This benefits *not only the stereotyped, but also his stereotyper.* The adjusted view helps to identify common denominators of the human condition. As the learner reaches out, to grow and change, he understands himself better within a newly clarified perspective. Hopefully, such learning will encourage service to older people to be given with hope and compassion.

Irving Rosow has warned:

> "The crucial people in the aging problem are not the old, but the younger age groups, for it is the rest of us who determine the status and position of the old person in the social order. What is at stake for the future is not only the alienation of the young from the old, but the alienation of the young from each other and of man from man. There is no way out of this dilemma, for young or old, without a basic reordering of our na-

tional aspirations and values of which the aging problem is but a token. Anything less than this will see us concentrating on superficial symptoms, especially tangible ones like housing the aged, and nibbling at the tattered edges of our problems without penetrating to their heart."[8]

In our consideration of the various facets of modern aging and the scope of needs in the field, it is important to take a long-range view, as well as to set some short-range and immediate goals. In summary, they are suggested as:

Long Range

1. An improved social milieu that recognizes and meets needs of all partially dependent persons, the aged among them: a milieu that nourishes individual and social health and offers to each individual a constructive place in society.

2. A climate of intergenerational acceptance that provides roles for older people and prepares the young for their own senescence.

3. The accompanying social, political, and educational programs to implement and maintain such a milieu.

Short Range

1. Continuing changes in social policy to recognize the range of needs of the elderly and to involve them in all phases of planning and implementation of need-meeting services.

2. Changes in educational and training programs that would define a broader, more coordinated role for the service professions, freeing them to provide more appropriate, knowledgeable, and effective services.

Immediate Goals

1. Changes in social policy that would extend immediately needed services to the current aged generation: for example, continuity of physical and mental health care, necessary financial assistance, housing, implementation of findings of various research and demonstration programs, information, education services, and the like.

2. Enabling families to fulfill filial responsibilities without undue financial or emotional burdens.

3. The immediate "retooling" of existing programs (social, political, educational) wherever possible.

Premises of the Album

This "Album" is based on an explicit set of premises that suggest the following points of view about aging.

1. There is no single, definitive, universally accepted "theory of aging," nor even a unified body of knowledge. This is a function of the newness of the study of senescence as a phase of life and the consequent lag in research and in understanding the process of aging as it affects the individual, his family, and society as a whole.

2. Senescence, as a phase of individual existence, may encompass upward of three decades during which time both the individual and his circumstances may undergo various changes.

3. There are many patterns of aging, just as there are many individual life-styles.

4. The older person is in interaction with his environment just as is every other human being. He responds to stress, help, or support, just as does anyone else. He can change and learn.

5. A large number of older people are subjected to multiple stress circumstances (especially poverty, change, discontinuity, physical and psychosocial losses, and the imminence of death). Some of these stresses are related to growing old; others are related to the social circumstances surrounding the aging person in contemporary society; still others have been part of an individual's life-style.

6. The imminence of death is an important reality for the older person. Like any other life occurrence, its significance is related to the unique life-view and life-style of the individual.

7. A broad, flexible world view of aging is most useful to the practitioner. This would include:

(a) Viewing the aged as a heterogeneous group that shares common characteristics and needs, some known, some not yet understood. Some of these circumstances affect other age groups as well. For the aged, they may occur in clusters, with a number of stresses converging at one time. This qualitatively alters their impact on the individual, his family, and society as a whole.

(b) Viewing the older person as an individual living his senescence with some continuity and integrity of personal life-style.

(c) Viewing the problems of aging as multidimensional, requiring their in-depth exploration to assure the most human response.

(d) Viewing service approaches on an interdisciplinary and coordinated basis, with emphasis on the dignity, integrity, needs, and assets of the person to be served.

8. Concerns about aging relate not only to the current older population, but to present middle-aged and future generations as well. Social image is a factor to be considered and preparation for aging should begin earlier in life.

9. Social reorganization and delivery of services are needed for society as a whole, and they are also needed for older people.

10. Stereotypes, both positive and negative, do exist and detract from the dimension of an individual as a human being.

11. Stereotypes impede the broad world view of aging presented here as desirable. They affect the public's view of the aged person and his own self-image.

12. Stereotypes also influence members of the service professions and are reflected in their approaches and delivery of services to the aged.

13. There is a need for change in some aspects of professional service offerings to older people and their families. Some changes indicated are:

(a) Creative approaches in need-meeting; the development of new roles, perhaps even some new professions.

(b) An epidemiological approach.

(c) An integrated approach to need and service; this implies interdisciplinary cooperation.

14. The older adult himself must become more involved both in decision making and in providing services. Such involvement includes social and political, as well as personal, aspects.

15. A broader approach to services suggests the involvement, on new levels, of paraprofessionals and volunteers.

16. Educational programs must be revamped in recognition of these premises.

Some of these views are discussed in the ensuing sections and are dramatized in the vignettes.

The Challenge

"What is it like to be old?" and "When is a person 'old,' anyway?" These questions, simply asked, are not easily answered.

They challenge us—young and old alike—to share our knowledge and experience in developing useful answers. Some answers can be helpful to the immediate generation of old people, and others may be guideposts in the future.

Everyone in the course of his personal or professional life may expect to be called on to serve or work with an older person or his family. A quick look at census statistics is convincing.

In 1971, there were about 20 million Americans aged 65 and over.[1] It is estimated that by 1990, 10 million will be over 75.[2] Since 1900, these two age groups have grown faster than the total population.

In 1968, the life expectancy for a person over 75 averaged about nine years. We are told that if medical science can conquer cancer, stroke, heart, blood vessel, and kidney diseases, the life expectancy will be even longer.[3] Therefore, in the coming years, more young people than ever can expect to live to a "ripe old age."

The aged population is also increasing annually by one quarter million. This turnover constantly changes the composition of the aged group. "The newcomers to the aged bring with them a somewhat different life history, and somewhat different characteristics."[4]

This fact underscores the need for continuous learning about several key elements in a changing picture of contemporary aging: the group as a whole, the individuals, the changing world, its effects on people, and the constellation of problems.

Life is a process of maturation from one developmental stage to the next. At each stage, an individual looks to members of the next stage as his role models. He learns from them knowing that soon he, too, will be reaching that age and stage, and he prepares in some ways to enter it.

Growing old is a continuum of the life process. The term "older adult" may identify a person anywhere between the ages of 65 and 95 and even older. (In 1971, Social Security was paying benefits to 5000 centenarians![5]) Just as a person changes during his early life so, too, may he be expected to change during his later years. Obviously, a 65-year-old individual will be different from one in his nineties! Yet, too often, younger people tend to think of "being old" as a fixed state, static and unchanging, with limited possibilities for growth. This is a stereotyped, one-dimensional view that colors the younger person's understanding of older people and will affect his self-image in his own senescence. It is important for young people to develop a more realistic image of aging than stereotypes of this kind suggest.

Although aging, as a developmental phase of life, is less known, less explored, and less understood than others, we are learning a great deal all the time. It is clear, for example, that aging is a heterogeneous and very individual process. That is, each person grows old in a different way. The differences will vary, depending on factors such as individual health, income, family circumstances, and personality; in short, on the individual and all the circumstances that shaped him until this point in his life.

The aged are not a homogeneous group. In our pluralistic society with its emphasis on individual adaptation, aging individuals have developed varied patterns to cope with the challenges of their older years.

Older people in this country represent a range of life-styles and patterns of living. Some are active, alert, and well, living and functioning in their own homes and communities. Others, not so active, alert, or well, still struggle to maintain their continuity of life-style. Some blind, ill, or handicapped aged people reside in institutions; others live in the community. Some active, ambulatory aged people, for one reason or another, elect to live in a "home for the aged." Others, some of whom may be almost as healthy, are institutionalized through no real choice of their own.

Therefore, when we attempt to serve an older person, we must see him as an individual, in his unique situation, within the context of his personal life-style.

Also, almost all aged people, at some point or another in senescence, share some common concerns. As a phase of life, aging presents a series of challenges (usually involving change and crisis) with which the individual must cope to survive and function. This fact holds true for all phases of life. Senescence, however, occurs within a rather negative sociocultural milieu at a point in life when a person may be least able to cope with the *clusters* of stress and crisis situations that may occur. For some older people, the changes may be gradual and gentle. For others, they may be traumatic and sudden. For almost all older people, however, this stage of life offers a series of losses. They are:

1. Loss of social identity (which may include loss of work role, identity losses related to changes in family roles, and the like).

2. Loss of sexual identity.

3. Losses in income.

4. Losses in health and physical capacities.

5. Losses in relationships: gradual isolation and aloneness.

6. Fear of death—an ever-present reality for the older person.[6]

These shared circumstances of older people suggest that there are concerns that characterize this phase of life as being different from earlier ones. This perception also, unless carefully considered, affects our attitude toward the aged person. For example, most older men must cope with the problems of rolelessness after retirement. Whereas a younger person maybe considered "employable but unemployed," the tendency is to consider the older one, "unemployable and retired." This poses a different and special problem for the older man as a function of his age (as well as of the employment scene). Similarly, whereas a younger widow may be expected to remarry and rebuild her life in some semblance of its original pattern, the same expectation does not apply to the aged widow.

It is also true that very large groups of aged people must cope with circumstances that also affect other age groups and that concern the entire community. For example, general conditions of poverty affect large groups of aged people.

> "The aged (75 plus) are definitely a low income group, underrepresented in the labor force; overrepresented in assistance recipients; highly dependent on Social Security but at lower benefit levels than younger groups of people."[7]

In general, of the 20 million older Americans, almost one half are living in or near the poverty level. (Only 10 percent have an income of $10,000 per year or more.) About 60 percent of this group are women, and 70 percent of these women are widows. The overwhelming majority of the aged live in the community. Most of them live with family or relations, but many of them (one fifth of the men and one third of the women) live all alone.[8]

The circumstances of poverty are not unique to old people. They are shared with other large sections of the population. This fact cannot be stressed too strongly, or we may begin to view important matters such as housing, income, health, and socialization as needs of older people only. In reality, they are concerns of our entire society. What *may be unique* for older people are some *special needs* in these and other areas, related to the unique circumstances of aging; and, also, some *special ways* that might most suitably be developed to meet these needs. Even then, some such solutions or services are often found to benefit other groups of people. For example, a community shopping service, often needed by older people, would be helpful to the chronically ill or handicapped person in the community, to a convalescing adult, and even to a young mother with a sick baby.

In short, an older person faces a *special set of problems* related to growing old, as well as *some general ones* in common with others. He requires an individualized view of himself as a unique person, different from anyone else. He should be viewed also as a member of a population group with a special set of needs, and he must be considered as a member of the total society sharing its broadest concerns.

This view mandates a flexible, open concept of aging in modern times and the need to understand and serve each older person within a broad but individualized frame of reference.

Summary

Society as a whole is challenged to adjust its view of senescence. We are encountering increasing numbers of aged in all our professional practices, in our communities, and within our own families. Yet we are relatively unprepared for its circumstances and its challenges.

Some circumstances of aging suggest a sense of despair, gloom, and pessimism. The knowledge that death lies at the end of the road frightens many people—young and old. These feelings and fears tend to immobilize us, to distort our view of aging and, indeed, our entire perspective of life. Yet, as others have put it,—one dies young or lives to be old. The implications of this choice are manifold to each of us as human beings.

The World of the Aging Person

Every person is born into and matures within a physical-social-emotional environment that offers certain opportunities to grow and function, and withholds others. Like everyone else, the aging person continues to interact with his environment, its value system and social organization, and with the people around him. The modern world of unrest and social change mandates a rethinking of some prevalent social concepts, some of which conflict with the realities of contemporary life.

The Work Ethic and Idea of Independence

The social value system is an active force in any person's environment. It helps to direct his life through setting goals and expectations and through shaping his social-and-self-image as a member of his society.

Inherent in the American value system is the Protestant work ethic which suggests that all able-bodied people should work, and that work should be the core of an individual's existence. Efficiency and productivity are regarded as virtues in our world. Idleness is equated with worthlessness, almost sinfulness. Success is measured by status, affluence, power, and productivity.

Independence, strongly flavored with the characteristics of "rugged individualism," is another prized value in the modern world. Together, these values prescribe the independent achiever as the preferred personality model. Conversely, any form of dependency reduces the social stature and individual worth of a person.

This social prescription for individual success has been a powerful influence on the current aged generation, which was born about or before the turn of this century. Yet, these values derived from a much earlier period in history when they represented a progressive change in social thinking—from judging individual worth on the basis of lineage with nobility as the criterion. That is, the opening of economic and political opportunities to the "common man," and the emergence of democratic forms encouraged a value system that emphasized individual effort over genealogy and productivity over inheritance.

Now, in an automated era, we are struggling with some contradictions arising from new circumstances. Brotman notes:

> "It is a particularly frustrating irony that progress in man's search for a longer life should produce the 'problems of aging.' In fact, the very successes in economic, social, medical and industrial 'progress' that now permit such a large proportion of our population to reach old age, also have produced changes that make the elderly a generally 'dependent' group and have robbed them of their most important and traditional functions, roles and status."[1]

Retirement and Some of Its Implications

This conflict applies directly to the aged person and his enforced retirement, as well as to younger individuals who cannot find work. In modern times, retirement is a fact of life usually mandated for most people at or about the age of 65. It has numerous implications for the individual, his family, and his world. For some people, retirement introduces a new phase of life offering long-awaited opportunities for pleasant uses of long-awaited leisure time. For most of the current aged generation, however, retirement is filled with difficult adjustments to drastically altered circumstances. A shattering change is the need to live on a fixed and usually reduced income. "When people retire [usually] their income drop by 60 to 80 percent."[2]

Many older people live in or close to poverty. Project Find reports that "poverty is a way of life for 3 out of 10 people 65 and over, in contrast to 1 out of 9 younger people."[3]

> "If we use as a measure of adequacy, the Bureau of Labor's statistics budget for an elderly couple described as modest but adequate . . . we find that more than 40 percent of the aged living in the community fall below this modest level of living."[4]

Finances are a problem for most older people, even those who do not live in poverty. Living on a fixed income under inflationary conditions imposes an economic handicap. Property and medical costs have consistently risen. For the elderly, the effects of these rises are compounded by their special circumstances. For example, two thirds of older Americans own their own homes. Many live in high tax zones, since they have lived there most of their lives, and the property values have risen.[5] Health care expenditures for an older person are three and one-half times those of younger people, and all of the public programs combined pay only two thirds of the bill.[6]

Furthermore, social legislation, prevailing attitudes (such as discriminatory hiring practices) and other individual circumstances, deprive older people of opportunities to meet their needs more adequately. For example, early retirement (at age 62) often affects workers who are not likely to have other sources of income. The "retirement test" does not permit an older person to earn more than a stipulated annual amount. If he is well enough and can find work itself a question in view of discriminatory hiring practices, he can learn only this amount before his social security benefits are cut at the rate of one dollar for every two dollars earned. Clearly, the fact of retirement is common to the world of almost all old people. For many, economic difficulty and deprivation are accompaniments.

However, the economic change is only one implication of retirement. Forced retirement carries with it a number of other stresses. In a climate prizing work and productivity, the nonproducer is an individual of second-class status. Lowy points out that, "Our society accords the highest status to those individuals who participate in the work roles which society has clearly defined . . . his who-ness is determined by what he does."[7]

The loss of work role, therefore, also affects the status, and social and self-image of the retiree and exacerbates his identity problems. This loss is also accompanied by a loss of social relationships established through the work situation. This connotes removal from an important reference group, related roles, changes in social patterns and a loosening of ties—all representing losses in sources of life satisfaction.

For many, retirement offers an abrupt change in life-style. Suddenly there is no need to rise, dress, and leave home at a given time for a given purpose. Feelings of uselessness accompany a search for alternatives. For the unprepared retiree, there are indeed few. He finds himself moving from a recognized and established position and pattern of life into a relatively uncertain one that lacks prestige. This holds true for both men and women.

Widowhood

The special circumstances of older women should be noted. Thirty-one out of every 100 people over 65 are widows (29 of whom are living alone or in homes of their own.) Close to 60 percent of them live in poverty.[8] Riley advises that, "the onset of widowhood has come increasingly later in life as more and more husbands and wives have survived together through the middle years.''[9] Yet, despite the gradual postponement of widowhood, most of these women have many years of life ahead of them. One half of the women widowed at age 65 can expect to live 15 years more and one third can look forward to 20.

The death of a spouse removes not only one's sexual partner, but one's partner in most life activities. Lopata advises that "most older widows showed limited involvement with their communities (except religious). In general, the older widow lives within a very small social space."[10] Older widows are often unprepared for the stressful aspects of the changes wrought by widowhood. Sadness and depression may be prolonged. "While widowhood suggests the need to develop new roles and relationships, modern conditions of population change tend to make such opportunities less and less available while the older widows lack the skill to replace them. This situation . . . points up the societal failure to socialize its members sufficiently so that they may acquire competence in maintaining old and building new interpersonal relationships."[11]

Change, Urban Living and Family Life

The world of the older person is also shaped by the industrialization and automation that have changed the world in many ways, including the development of cities and the changes in transportation and communication, in community life, and in family patterns.

Urban living mandates small homes and apartments for most people and affects the living arrangements of older people. In response, families have adopted a variety of patterns. Sometimes older parents continue to live near their offspring. Sometimes they live within an hour's ride. Sometimes they are separated by enormous geographical distances. In each case, obviously, relationships are differently patterned.[12]

There has been much speculation about the changing relationships between older people and their families. Ideas range from "families don't care" to "families are overburdened." Blenkner highlights the struggle of old people and their families to cope together with progressive changes:

> "Typically, the old person remains in his own abode as long as he is capable of self-care. However, children or other relatives increasingly take on or assist with the heavier tasks of housekeeping and home maintenance, provide transportation and escort, manage illness and in general watch over him, substituting their strengths, mobility and judgment for his declining abilities. As he becomes more frail, he is likely to move into the home of a relative where more personal care and protective supervision can be given. Only a small minority are institutionalized, and then only when the demand for intensive and skilled care rises beyond the capacity of family members.
>
> "These too are sensible and valid solutions up to a point; but if car-

ried too far they become destructive to both the old and their kin. An excessive burden can so overwhelm a family as to actually endanger its members' physical, emotional and social stability, or else result in a complete irreversible rejection of the old person with all the accompanying guilt and suffering."[13]

The move of many younger families to suburbia has often left an older parent behind in his old apartment or home. Concurrently, the vacated homes and apartments have become occupied by new population groups, often of a sociocultural or ethnic background different from the original group. Older people remain socially isolated within their own neighborhoods; strangers among a new population of younger families who may speak a different language, eat different foods, and live in a different life-style. The "old neighborhood" has changed. Small shops have changed hands and their proprietors have moved away. In their place are the impersonal supermarkets usually carrying items preferred by the newcomers of the community. Even many social and religious institutions have changed hands or left the community, further depriving the older person of familiar relationships.[14] The aged inhabitant of just such a community, Strawberry Mansion in Philadelphia, is described this way:

> "If we try to construct a picture of his life-style, we would see the Strawberry Mansioner as a person with more than his share of physical, economic and social handicaps. As he engages in everyday necessary coping behavior, he performs at an average level in spite of his lesser resources. However, where the behavor is elective, rather than necessary to his self-maintenance, he conserves energy. Thus, he engages in fewer social and self-actualizing behaviors. He ascribes much of his difficulty to his location in an extremely noxious environment. However, where a person with many opportunities would get out of the environment, the SM dweller does not. At least one major reason . . . is that his very low rent or homeownership together with his low income, lock him in. His life space is grossly restricted, ordinary coping behavior requires energy expenditure at a near upper-threshold level and he cannot escape. Lowered morale is the inevitable result of any of these antecedent factors taken separately, and particularly of the interaction among them."[15]

In both urban and rural areas, 28 out of 100 aged people live alone. Some of them are "lost" or "invisible." Many are poor. Many are lonely. All endure hardships in a harsh environment.

Project FIND describes "How the Elderly Poor Got Lost":

> "It was necessary to FIND the elderly poor persons. Some were truly lost. They lived on mountain or prairie roads which led nowhere. Others were lost in cities even to the census taker. Persons residing in 'hotels'

are presumed to be transient and they are not included even in the nation's decennial counting of its citizens. Some were not so much lost as invisible, because nobody wanted to look. If too many of them frequented a cafeteria where food was low in cost and it was possible to sit for a long time over a cup of coffee and a roll, young people began to go elsewhere to eat, repelled by the sight of arthritic hands carefully counting out coins, dragging feet and clothes unkempt or clumsily restyled. . . . To many of today's indigent aged, to be poor and alone is to be ashamed. Many had become invisible by their own wish."[16]

Of the city dweller, Cowan writes:

"The rooms that old people can afford are rarely cozy refuges. In the hotels and rooming houses of the West side, they often have to share the bath with junkies or winos. Many think of themselves as prisoners in furnished cells, too frightened to go out unless absolutely necessary. . . . Living alone and poor, many old people don't care too much about eating . . . there are thousands who still feel lonely and useless."[17]

Not only the poor elderly are affected by urban and rural change.

"In predominantly low income areas, some elderly persons were found to be relatively well-to-do. Often, these persons are left over from a more prosperous neighborhood past. . . . These elderly people are often out of touch with their new neighbors. They often need help with daily living."[18]

The move to the cities has left many older people isolated in rural areas as well.

"Older people are isolated from one another and invisible to the community. Their problems are hidden with them and attention to these problems is slow in coming. The population of older people in rural areas has increased, while the overall growth of the areas has stopped.

"When stores and services close, no new ones replace them. . . . the problem is particularly serious when doctors give up longtime practices . . . poverty is a problem for older people in rural areas . . . dilapidated structures and high property taxes are the basis of severe housing difficulties . . . there may not be running water in some areas . . . the transportation problem is extreme for those who don't drive cars."[19]

These are some of the unique ways in which the changing scene has affected old people.

The Concept of Interdependence

The changing world also invites a reexamination of our social values. How "ruggedly individualistic," how independent can one continue to be when he must depend on social networks for his daily food, for traveling to work, for his own and family's health, for his children's education, and future welfare? Industrialism reinforces the concept of *community interdependence* —with a concurrent shift in our social definition of independence and dependence.

Kalish indicates:

"Traditional views regarding independence and dependence have deep roots in the United States and other western nations. These views probably have encouraged many of the advances in our country. That these same views may also be unduly harmful to the well being of the elderly and other persons who require a variety of all kinds of community and personal support is often ignored."[20]

The development of communal interdependence is reflected in the institutionalization of many functions originally handled through the family. This applies to old as well as to young people. Discussing "Normal Dependencies of Aging," Blenkner addresses

". . . dependency as a state of being; not as a state of mind, a state of being in which to be old, as to be young, is to be dependent. Such dependency is not pathological. . . . Under the impact of modern living conditions . . . there is a tremendous need to develop and expand imaginative and societal solutions to the normal dependencies of aging."[21]

These concerns are intensified for the elderly poor. Project FIND identifies the need "to organize a network of essential facilities and services to alleviate the social consequences . . . of low income and advanced age." FIND establishes priorities for health and medical care, information and outreach services, nutrition, housing, and transportation service to counter conditions of isolation and loneliness. Almost any one of the 20 million elderly people would profit from, at least, one, and probably more than one, of these services.[22]

Summary

Clearly many Americans grow old within a harsh environment that is neither aware of, prepared for, nor organized toward meeting their needs. The social value system tends to denigrate their individual worth. Social organization ignores their growing dependency and offers limited opportunities to retain independence. For most elderly people, their social world and social opportunities are diminished. For a very large group who are poor, many physical necessities of life are inadequate or lacking.

Myths and Stereotypes in the World of the Aging Person

"*Myth*—legend or story, usually attempting to account for something in nature, . . . any invented story . . . an imaginary person or thing."

"*Stereotype* . . . a fixed form that never changes."

All societies develop myths about life and death. They derive from the world view of existence within a culture as an effort to explain and understand existential phenomena. Although social change and new knowledge may provide more appropriate explanations, these ideas often remain a fixed part of the conceptual world that is a powerful influence on social and individual life.

By definition, a stereotype—whether positive or negative—suggests a limited and stationary view. A progressive philosophy recognizing social change must, therefore, be aware of and reject the effects of stereotyped thinking on the ideological scene.

The average American grows older within an emotional atmosphere riddled with myths and stereotypes about aging and old people. These myths range from positive to negative notions about aging. For example:

Positive: "The Tranquility Myth"

Old age is a time of relative peace and tranquility when people can relax and enjoy the fruits of their labor after the storms of life have passed. This is also known as the "myth of the golden years" or "the harvest years."

This extreme overlooks *the reality* that old age is a time of substantial stresses, especially those related to poverty, illness, and isolation. Often it is *these stresses* that produce the depression, anxiety, paranoia, and psychosomatic illnesses commonly associated with older patients and ascribed, in a stereotyped manner, to the aging process.[1]

Negative: "The Inevitability Myth"

"An older person thinks and moves slowly. He does not think of himself as well as he used to nor as creatively. He is bound to himself and to his past and can neither change nor grow. He can neither learn well nor swiftly and even if he could . . . he would not wish to. Tied to his personal traditions and growing conservatism, he dislikes innovations. . . . Not only can he not move forward, but he often moves backward, he enters a second childhood. . . . He becomes irritable and cantankerous, yet shallow and enfeebled. He lives in his past. He is behind the times. He is aimless of mind, wandering, reminiscing, and garrulous. Indeed, he is a study in decline; . . . the picture of mental and physical failure. He has lost and cannot replace friends, spouse, job, status, power, influence, income. He is often stricken by diseases. . . . His body shrinks and so too does the flow of blood to his brain. . . . enfeebled, uninteresting he awaits his death, a burden to society, to his family, and to himself."[2]

This "overdrawn picture" implies a number of preconceptions, for example, that all older people are similar, that aging involves various irreversible illnesses (mental or physical), a "fixed" state of mind, and shrinking capacities, and that an aged person is ipso facto, rigid, unchangeable, sterile, and dependent.

Such views about aging have affected all levels of public thinking including the older person's self-image which derives, in part, from society's view of him.

Riley challenges these views with the caution that:

"Scholars often make inferences about how individuals age directly from the cross-section societal picture. The older person, qua member of society, tends to become comparatively disadvantaged in many respects, despite the various qualifications and mitigating factors. . . . In the more dramatic accounts, all these tendencies seemingly add up to a tragic stereotype of the older person as destitute, ill, facing irreparable losses, no longer integrated into society and no longer subject to society's controls and sanctions. Old age appears as a nadir; the end of a long decline. . . . How then do the actual data on aging individuals compare with such suppositions? A glance at the scattered available clues shows a picture that is, in certain respects, at sharp variance with the stereotype. The older worker's productivity shows no consistent decline. Scholarship is maintained at a fairly high level into old age. There is little evidence that aging brings sexual impotence. The typical older person seems to have a strong sense of his own worth, to minimize his self-doubts, and not even to regard himself as old."[3]

Every field has its myths and stereotypes about the limitations of the aged person and the inevitability and irreversibility of his conditions and circumstances. Since a person's ideas affect his entire approach to the service he gives, these incorrect views about aging must be corrected if we are to improve our understanding of the older person and our services on his behalf.

Views of this kind and their negative effects on the services of some professionals underlie comments like the following.

The Physician.   "No sense to try any therapy on Mr. D. He's too old (age 86)," or "She'll probably never be out of the wheelchair."

The Nurse.   "They're just like little children . . . you have to coddle them," or ". . . besides, she doesn't really know what she is doing."

The Social Worker.   "How can you work with the aged? Isn't it awfully depressing?" or "I prefer to work with younger adults or children. The prognosis is so much more hopeful than with elderly."[4]

Such expressions stem from underlying misconceptions that reflect implicit, or even unconscious, acceptance of the myths about aging that exist in different fields. Some of them are:

Biological Myths

These myths view aging as a degenerative biological process that is accompanied by inevitable illness and breakdown which "should not be tinkered with because the way it is now is the way nature is."[5]

This view may well influence a nurse, doctor, physiotherapist, or dentist, to shrug his shoulders and say: "What do you expect? This is caused by aging." "This" may refer to the illness, pain, disability, incontinence, or any other condition that the professional *assumes* to be unchangeable because of age.

The *realities* are highlighted by knowledge and experience that contradict these views. Shanas explains that while it is true that senescence is a period of general physiological decline,

> "There is agreement among geriatricians that physiological changes are highly individual; and that there is a wide range of therapeutic and medical treatment to serve older people, to alleviate physical distress, to mitigate effects of illness, to offer rehabilitative services, to reverse certain correctible conditions."[6]

Older people's physical circumstances are not uniformly inevitable or irreversible but are amenable to medical, surgical, psychiatric, and other kinds of treatment intervention. Breslow says:

> "It is as important to foster the idea of good health in the later decades of life as it is to advise people how to prevent sickness. Most of us . . . still adhere to the notion that sickness and disability are 'natural' consequences of aging. We need rather to promote the ideal of being healthy into old age."[7]

Psychological Myths

These suggest such "inevitabilities" as memory loss, the inability to learn or perform new tasks, and a lack of capacity for self-help, decision-making, or problem solving.

The realities, as presented by a number of psychologists, are that chronological aging alone does not account for such changes but, instead, that they are connected with a number of other life circumstances. The interrelationship of psychological and physical health is important.

Oberleder stresses the fact that "psychologically, the sick old person is more like the sick young person than he is like the well old person." The effects of health and illness on the older person's psychological functioning cannot be stressed enough, she reports.

As for mental decline, "actually, according to intelligence test results," Oberleder continues "there is really only a very slight decline in the mental function of the elderly, and many functions, such as vocabulary, practical reasoning and special skills in which the person remains actively engaged, often improve with age."[8] She observes:

> "Social and psychological factors and individual frustrations, and particularly the effects of ill health must all be factors in any consideration of the mental and personality characteristics of an older person, otherwise, most of the stereotyped theories about aging, especially the stereotype 'senility' are bound to be right. This is particularly true of the elderly patient who is very often seen in an emergency state . . . People in panic conform to the negative stereotypes (adolescents too)."

The effects of environmental stress are related to the psychological state. Arsenian points out, ". . . every person has a 'breaking point' . . . influenced by critical events in living, their timing, and . . . cumulative and counteractive effects." He analyzes the various stresses that affect the older person, as a result of the changes in his environment and the diminished opportunities for satisfaction, pointing out that older people may become increasingly powerless in the control of their destinies. This circumstance is closely connected with psychological breakdowns and losses.[9]

Psychiatric Myths

These include the "brain damage myth" and the "unresponsive to therapy myth."

Myth: the brain damage myth. All people have damage to the brain as a consequence of aging.

Reality: "Senility" is not inevitable. Two conditions, cerebral arteriosclerosis and senile brain disease create brain conditions, as in younger people. Neither brain damage nor aging account for the occurence of [all] mental conditions among older people.

Myth: The unresponsive-to-therapy myth. Older people are not treatable because their mental conditions are irreversible. Their mental disorders are primarily physical and, therefore, beyond the scope of psychiatric treatment.

Reality: Many mental and emotional disorders affecting older people can be treated. To a notable extent, they are reversible. Under reasonably good circumstances, more older psychiatric patients improve or recover than fail to react to psychotherapy. Older people in group therapy also respond positively.[10]

Furthermore, we are advised that a "senile pattern of brain deterioration does not commonly accompany advancing age; when it does occur it is likely to be pathological rather than a normal concomittant of growing old."[11]

The Group for Advancement of Psychiatry urges:

"The aims of psychiatric treatment . . . are to decrease personal suffering . . . and in general to improve the patients' functioning to the maximum possible extent. The prognosis will depend less on the age of the patient than on the severity of his brain syndrome, the rigidity and type of his character structure, the extent of physical impairment and the availability of needed therapeutic, economic and social resources.

Few older patients are truly rigid, unchangeable, stubbornly negatitistic or unresponsive to skilled concern."[12]

Social Senility Myths

These myths suggest the inevitability of certain kinds of socially unacceptable behavior as a predetermined component of aging. A sad and serious accompaniment to these social myths is the unrealistic expectation, by many, of what behavior may be deemed socially acceptable for an older person. The expectation that he will act in socially unacceptable ways can prevent the identification of his possible need for help. Very often, psychosocial treatment is not given simply because the need, obscured by the stereotyped view, is not identified. For example, if it is expected and accepted that an older person, *only* because of his age, will be cranky, angry, impatient, and forgetful, then it follows that helpful intervention may not be considered appropriate or necessary.

In reality, it has been demonstrated through socialization programs such as remotivation, reality orientation, and group therapy as well as individual counseling that many old people can and do respond to appropriate social treatment.

Myths of Unproductivity

These suggest that, at an arbitrary age, older people become unproductive, decline, disengage themselves from life, and prefer to live in a state of withdrawal and segregation.

In reality, assuming the absence of disease and social adversity, older people remain actively concerned about and involved in their personal and community relationships. They exhibit normal capacities to "handle their own business." Older people need opportunities to make choices, including the choice and opportunity to remain within the mainstream of life.

Myth of "Sexual Senility"

This is a common misconception that the older person has lost his sexual drive. This myth intensifies the view of him as arid and unproductive, robs him of sexual identity, and limits the perception of him as a whole person. It lies buried in comments such as, "Aren't they cute?" when two older people exhibit normal heterosexual behavior.

The reality is that

> "Sexual needs and desires do not undergo an abrupt change with advancing years. The sex organs change more than do the individual's sexual needs. The capacity for reproduction ebbs more rapidly than does the sexual desire. Abrupt loss of desire is generally symptomatic of psychological factors.
>
> "However, society, including the aged, lacks general understanding of sexual urges, capacities and expression in older people. Social conditioning is a particularly important factor in the sexual attitudes and practices of older persons. . . . Well-adjusted persons do not have sexual problems because of aging."[13]

Oberleder suggests further that, "Impulse gratification of this most basic kind is probably necessary for survival. . . . The need to deny emotions automatically cuts off libidinal drive. Making emotions possible in older age will go a long way toward cutting down the incidence of senile psychosis."[14]

In fact, 66.8 percent of the older men live in their own homes with their spouses[15] and, "In an average year, there will be almost 2000 blushing seventy-five-plus brides and more than 6000 seventy-five-plus grooms going to the altar."[16]

Family Myths

They suggest that "families don't care" and that they "discard their elderly relatives." This one-dimensional, negative view of family relationships is extremely dysfunctional and results in skewed judgments about old people, their families, and their circumstances.

The reality is that families have developed various relationship patterns with their older adult members.

"In a careful study on the utilization of state hospitals in New York," reports Busse, "Goldfarb concludes that elderly patients who are admitted are 'not persons who have been rejected by their families for financial or social reasons. They are sick people who need comprehensive care and for whom no other community facility is yet available.' "[17]

Old people are often brought to, or remain in institutions because there are no community facilities to meet their partial dependency needs; hence, they are institutionalized because the alternatives offered by the community are limited or are nil. Similarly, many old people do show physical improvement in nursing homes and extended care facilities. However, by the time that they are ready to be discharged, they may be forced to remain institutionalized for various reasons, usually because their new partial dependency needs cannot be met in the community. Thus, time and money factors combine with inadequate community resources to keep many people institutionalized who might otherwise return to the community and who might continue to function at home with some help.

Butler reports

". . . more disabled and even bedridden older people are cared for by families than are cared for in all types of institutions. Families supply more services to their aged relatives than are supplied by community agencies. However, they often do this at great cost to themselves which is not desirable for them or for their own families or for the older person. Many families could continue to help if they had some relief. Respite services are needed."[18]

The myths of "role reversal" or "second childhood" bear scrutiny. Brody states:

"There can be no true role reversal and no second childhood . . . the behavior of a sick, brain-damaged old person may appear childlike, but he is not a child. Half a century or more of adulthood cannot be wiped out; though some areas of memory . . . may be eroded, there can be no consistent return to a previous level."[19]

As for role reversal, Blenkner points out that part of maturity involves the adult's capacity to be depended on by the aged parent. . . . This is not role reversal, she says, but fulfillment of the filial role, and implies resolution of earlier maturational phases.[20]

In view of so much knowledge that contradicts the popular myths and stereotypes of aging, how is it that misconceptions prevail? One reason is that new knowledge is inadequately communicated or shared on all levels, among professionals or with the public. Another is the inadequacy of interpretation to the public at large. These communication gaps affect the members of the public who enter the service professions, and whose understanding reflects the limitations of the total population. Still another reason is that service professionals tend to see old people and their families at points when they need some sort of help, or in times of emergency or crisis. People seek out doctors, psychiatrists, nurses, and social workers at points of illness and crisis. Shanas suggests that the staff of social agencies, in the recent past, believed that their elderly clients were representative samples of the aged population and that, on this basis, they developed some of their stereotyped concepts of old people. However, when they analyzed their client population, they found that these older clients were apt to be more destitute, childless, widowed, and so forth. In short, their clients had fewer resources than other old people and, hence, came to social agencies for help.[21]

Summary

The myths and stereotypes described here are part of the world in which Americans grow and grow old. They affect the social image of aging, the self-image of the aged person, and the attitudes and activities of those who deal with him. They are not helpful, since they are distortions or exaggerations of realities that prevent a clear view of the road to services.

Service professions are challenged to find the most constructive path through the maze of myths. If we focus only on problems, we may well realize all the stereotypes through self-fulfilling prophecies, reinforcing the hopeless view of aging as a dependent, arid phase of life. If we focus only on the positive potentials, without clear assessment of need, we are led down the primrose path of the "Golden Years" myth. What we need is a soberly balanced view of people growing old—with a clear understanding of both their assets and needs.

Problems and Tasks of the Individual in Senescence

The social and sociological worlds of a person comprise two dimensions of his existence. His inner being and emotional concerns are a third dimension.

During each phase of his life, an individual copes with the demands of his environment and of his own developing personality. At different times, these demands will differ in accord with altered circumstances, environmental and intrapsychic. The maturing personality continues to master his techniques of dealing with life through the performance of these developmental tasks.

In general, a person grows with some integrity of personality and in keeping with an evolving life-style. Older individuals have developed their coping mechanisms through a lifetime of effort and experience, and are most likely to continue to employ those that have seemed most effective.

Yet the new demands of senescence do require alterations in these methods, and even the development of some new coping techniques.

Although aging is different for everyone, depending on his circumstances, this phase of life, like any other, is characterized by common dynamics that cut across socioeconomic and ethnic lines. Each person is challenged individually.

Erikson offers a good point at which to begin to consider the developmental tasks of the aging person. He describes each stage of life in terms of crises, or tasks, the successful solution of which leads to health, while failure leads to pathology. He believes this sequence to be universal. The typical solution of the tasks and crises depends on the sociocultural environment in which the individual operates.

Erikson describes the last great developmental crisis as "the fruit of the 7 stages."

> "I know of no better word for it than integrity . . . the acceptance of one's own and only life cycle. . . . It means a different love of one's parents, free of the wish that they should have been different, and acceptance of the fact that one's life is one's own responsibility. It is a sense of comradeship with men and women of different times and of different pursuits, who have created orders and objects and sayings conveying human dignity and love . . . he knows that an individual life is the accidental coincidence of but one life cycle with but one segment of history and that for him, all human integrity stands and falls with the one style of integrity of which he partakes."[1]

The modern aged person performs his developmental tasks with consideration for the range of changes, discontinuities, unpreparedness and crises of his own life.

Change and Discontinuity

Whether the changes in his life represent loss or gain or both, the individual is required to cope with this process and with the new circumstances it mandates for him. In some way, he must assess the new situation and deal with it. The requirement to cope with life's demands characterizes maturation at each point of development. Child, adolescent, adult—each enters a new stage, learns its dimensions, and tries to deal with its implications. The very content of the changes in senescence offers unique, qualitative differences from the earlier stages.

Benedict has described the sharp discontinuities that mark the transitions of role expectation from childhood to adolescence to adulthood and old age.[2] She identifies the characteristics of differences in role expectations as responsible-nonresponsible, dominance-submission, and contrasted sex roles. Stein and Cloward suggest further that the transition to old age is most striking because of these characteristics in role change.[3]

For the aged person, these discontinuities may be experienced one at a time, or in combination. They may occur suddenly and traumatically, or in slow progressions. How they occur is also important. Therefore, both the discontinuities themselves, and the manner and circumstances under which they occur are considerations.

Some of these discontinuities which reduce the capacity of the older person to function in keeping with his lifelong patterns of responsibility, independence, and dominance are the following:

Physical and Biological Changes.   Many of these changes lead to diminished physical capacities and disabilities, and to health losses.

"Aging itself is not a disease and most older people are not in poor health. However, aging is accompanied by physical changes and increases the possibility of the development of chronic illnesses. Some of the more common chronic disease conditions among older people include diseases of heart, cancer, stroke, arthritis, influenza and pneumonia, diabetes, hypertension, and mental and nervous conditions."[4]

Physical medicine has identified a number of physical changes in older people that are common even in the absence of chronic disease. They include changes in skin, skeleton and muscles, the nervous system, and a decreasing acuity of hearing, vision, and other senses. They also include respiratory changes, digestive difficulties, and changes in temperature maintenance. As a result older individuals may have greater difficulty in coping with environmental stress and in adjusting to change. The risk of accidents is also increased. Nevertheless, Lawton notes:

"It has been observed that biologically, elderly humans do not differ appreciably from persons in other groups. Physiological, sensory, emotional and physical changes do occur but, *the immense reserves of the human body and the ingenious and often devious methods of compensation . . . allow them* (the elderly) *to function in this complex world with surprising success.*"[5]

Economic Discontinuities. Whether he has been a wealthy and powerful man who retires to a life of ease and pleasure; or whether he has been a hard-working man who retires to a fixed and reduced income on social security, the older person must cope with the changes presented by the circumstances of his retirement.

Social and Psychological Discontinuities. Changes and losses in roles and status (work role, sex role, and family and community roles), loss of friends, spouse, and other peers through their illness, death, institutionalization, and other circumstances are serious. Reduced opportunities for replenishing these losses may induce feelings of helplessness, isolation, depression, a poor self-image, and a threatened sense of self.

Death. This is a real *threat of discontinuity of life itself,* and its meaning is very different for each person. Death, as the end of life, is a reality for everyone. For the older person, however, it is a more imminent one, the awareness of which colors his view, affects his time perspective, and the planning of his daily life. His view may be optimistic, neutral, or pessimistic. He may admit, permit, or deny, depending on his own style. The need to cope with his own anticipation of his own death is one of the most pressing tasks of the older person.

Unpreparedness

The growing need to recognize and understand senescence points up both social and individual unpreparedness for this phase of existence. There have been avoidance and denial in preparing for aging that reflect both fear and ignorance about this stage of life.

Individual Unpreparedness for Aging. The younger person has role models of adulthood as the child had role models of adolescence. Each learns through the opportunity to study and to anticipate the new stage, to integrate some of its demands, and to prepare in some ways for the new role.

Today's older person has very few of these role models, and even few peers. He knows less of what lies ahead of him, and he sees fewer alternatives. He is much closer to the expectation of disabling circumstances, and to the finality of death. His understanding is circumscribed not only by his own inexperience, but by society's. For each stage of life before this one, there has been opportunity for some kind of formal or informal preparation through training or observation. But, as has been indicated, aging as a three-decade period is relatively new. The individual's opportunities to prepare for his own aging has been severely limited. As one 84-year-old man put it, "When I was young I expected to die at 50. I was astonished to find myself living beyond that age!"

Family Unpreparedness. The family's consternation at, and inability to cope with, some of the problems of its aging members presents practical and emotional repercussions for the older person. New dependency needs or other circumstances of his aging suggest altered familial relationships that the older person must understand and with which he must cope.

Social Unpreparedness. The lack of community preparation for the needs of partially dependent people (of any age) holds a constant and unique threat of traumatic change. For example, a younger person who is hospitalized usually has the realistic expectation of returning home after recovery. The older person, however, faces a far less certain future. His return to health is likely to take a much longer time, and during this period he may lose his home through a variety of possible contingencies (for example, he may be sent to a nursing home and may remain permanently institutionalized, even after he recovers). Such radical changes in his living arrangements are often beyond his control and contribute to his growing sense of powerlessness. Social unpreparedness extends to the helping professions which do not adequately prepare their workers to understand, advise, or help deal with the concerns of aged people and their families.

Crisis

The threat of crisis hangs severely over the older person. In some instances, the changes may have been gradual, so gradual as to have been almost imperceptible. Perhaps they were not understood, or they were ignored, or were denied. At some point, these gradual changes may culminate into a qualitatively new situation that takes on the proportion of a crisis. In other instances, the threats or possibilities occur suddenly.

Sudden illness, such as stroke, or the death of a spouse are serious and not uncommon crises for older people. Although they occur also at earlier periods in life, they are more likely to occur in senescence. Their implications for older people may be quite different than for younger, as they may mandate other life changes. Loss of a spouse may alter an older person's living arrangement. Loss of his physical capacities requires a whole series of adaptations, especially in the absence of family, caring person, helping agent, or adequate economic resources. Unpredictable changes in social policies, such as cuts in public assistance programs, changes in eligibility requirements, rent controls, and the like threaten the older person with crisis (as, indeed, they threaten others who are dependent on social welfare policies and practices).

Cluster of Circumstances. Finally, the *cluster of circumstances and the number of simultaneous changes* can compound the older person's problem.

For example, he may be required to cope, simultaneously, with his own waning physical capacities, the loss of a spouse, a changed living circumstance, a reduced income, and the loss of work role. The convergence of so many demands within a relatively short time span represents enormous stress and makes great demands on the individual.

Threat to Independence and Capacity To Control One's Destiny. The changes and losses in the individual, his surroundings and circumstances, threaten the older person with a reduced state of independence and diminished opportunity to exercise control over his existence. This introduces a new struggle to maintain one's independence as a mature individual in society.

The Quality of Loss Within the Changes. For all one's losses, one must have appropriate opportunity to mourn. When drastic changes occur, the older person needs a chance to express suitable emotions related to the meaning of these changes *to him.* The loss of spouse, of home, of limb, or perhaps only the loss of the familiar exchanged for something new (even when the new is better), all require recognition. It is important to permit mourning and allow for the *time* it requires. Just as physical healing may be slower in an older person, so emotional healing may take longer. Such a time allowance enables the person to assess the realities of his changed circumstances, and gives him a "breather" before he assumes the burdens of their new demands. When opportunities for such mourning are limited or denied, the emotional energy may be poured into angry or depressive reactions.

The meaning of time is different for older people. On a daily basis, an older person may have "too much time." From the long-range view, he may have "too little." This conflict between his two time perspectives affects his feelings, actions, and coping capacities.

Developmental Tasks

The tasks of senescence, like those of the earlier life stages, are performed within the matrix of a person's inner existence and outer world.

The older person is challenged with both maintenance and change tasks. Buhler says:

"In every human being there are 4 tendencies in operation at all times. These are need satisfaction (maintenance); adaptive self-imitation (change); creative expansion (change); upholding internal order (maintenance). A primary task for the old person is the need to rethink his reasons for being; his philosophy of life; to reassess himself; consider his past and his future."[6]

Buhler considers the self-assessment of this period to be very different from that of earlier periods.

"It is much more serious . . . because it takes place with awareness of this being a critical period, a last moment for making changes, for improving on the results, for bringing in some of the harvest everybody is hoping for."[7]

Intimately connected with the question, "What am I living for?" for which the older person must find some answers, is the question, "Who am I?" Thus the older person begins to redefine his identity in terms of his altered circumstances.

Anderson and Clarke list five adaptive tasks for older people:

1. *Perception of aging and definition of instrumental limitations.* That is, an awareness and acceptance of changes with acknowledgement that certain activities can no longer be pursued as successfully as they were in younger life.

2. *Redefinition of physical and social life space.* This means redefining the boundaries of one's life activities. The capacity to do this arises directly from the first task, for when a person recognizes his limitations, he can then draw the realistic boundaries.

3. *Substitution of alternative sources of need-satisfaction.* This requires a willingness and ability to engage in new, feasible pursuits. It also implies the presence of alternatives in his environment.

4. *Reassessment of criteria for evaluating self.*

5. *Reintegration of values and life goals.* He must find ways for his life to have meaning and purpose to him.[8]

In this process, a person needs to know that he *can adapt, can change,* and *can learn*—a view of himself that is often denied him by his social and self-image.

Peck suggests the following three developmental tasks of old age:

1. *Ego-differential versus work-role preoccupation.* "Am I a worthwhile person only insofar as I can do a full-time job—or because of the kind of person I am?"

2. *Body Transcendence versus body preoccupation.* This requires a redefinition of "happiness" and "comfort" to handle the various declines in physical powers that are likely to develop.

3. *Ego-transcendence versus ego preoccupation.* This task is concerned with some positive adaptation to the certainty of death.[9]

This last suggests the final significantly different developmental task of the aged person, that is, preparation for his own death. That preparation is integrally bound with the performance of the earlier tasks described. A person who has defined himself, made peace with life, has integrated changes, and "overcome" the difficulties of senescence has already made ready for his death in many ways. Since, however, these tasks are rarely completed (although more often dealt with than younger people tend to imagine), there does need to be a conscious working toward acceptance of the end of life.

Both Buhler and Peck suggest the need for finding an inner fulfillment, an inner meaning, a sense of having made "peace with life"—whatever that life may have been or may be for the individual.

Of course, these views represent ideal goals. Few individuals perform these "tasks" to complete perfection at any point in their lives.

Summary

All old people must cope with changes, many of which represent loss. The developmental tasks of senescence are performed within its unique circumstances of discontinuity, unpreparedness (individual, family, and social), threat of crisis, lack of resources, inadequate alternatives, diminished power, qualitative change in the meaning of life and time, pressure of death, and the convergence of many stress factors.

Developmental tasks involve rethinking one's individual perceptions of the meaning of life, of one's identity, and the retooling of capacities to meet the demands of new situations most effectively. All old people are called upon to perform these tasks as part of the developmental process of senescence.

Part II
An Album of Vignettes

Life Work and Death

In the End

In the end you are all alone
And only yourself is with you
And what once you had given is nothing—
Only what you give now.

In the end, if you've lived alone,
And your spirit is hungry and thirsty
You will find there is little to feed
The soul that is left in need.

In the end, if you've lived with loving
And your heart has not been cheated—
Then when you're all alone
Perhaps
Then you'll not be depleted.

Shura Saul

Aunt Becky

"Listen, Aunt Becky," Rita said seriously. "I want you to think about moving to another apartment. Your legs aren't getting any better—you have to stop climbing three flights of stairs."

Becky Brown stirred impatiently. "Where will I move?" she retorted with some anger. "Here I'm paying $65 a month for four rooms. Where will I get such a low-rent apartment? I can't afford to pay any more than that. Besides, your Uncle Bob wouldn't be happy anywhere else. I know he'll give me a hard time if I say I want to move."

Rita sighed as she looked around the dingy, old apartment. Aunt Becky had done her best to make it cheerful. Prints and pictures rested, somewhat crookedly, against the dirty walls; magazines in gay colors were stacked untidily on the bookshelves. Although she had no children of her own, Aunt Becky had been a baby nurse. The house was cluttered with snapshots of "her babies"—at all stages of their development, from infancy to marriage. She had retained contact with many of the families for whom she had worked. It had been a happy job, helping the young mothers care for their newborn babies; teaching them the small practical things that made mothering more fun, less burdensome. Aunt Becky had taken no courses—but she had brought the folk lore and lessons of a lifetime of hard work. And she always had a joke or story to drive the lessons home. Her apartment bore a happy, lopsided grin —much like her own easy, hearty laughter.

But the window blinds were dusty . . . the windows streaked with dirt . . . the paint peeling . . . the faded old curtains beginning to tear. Aunt Becky's housekeeping was severely limited by her increasing and numerous physical infirmities.

Becky followed her niece's eyes around the room. "I know," she said, "it looks pretty rundown to you. But to Uncle Bob and me, it's home."

"But—Aunt Becky—."

Becky interrupted. "Okay, okay, my dear," she said, "I promise to think about it."

Uncle Bob had retired years ago. That is, he had been retired. They let him work until he was 80 years old. (How much longer, they had said to him, did he think they'd be able to keep him?) He was almost 90 now. A thin, wiry man—he had kept up his own morale by the simple expedient of refusing to alter his lifelong daily routine. He would leave the house each morning to go "downtown"—even though he had no job to go to. He spent his days in the public squares, the parks, sometimes a library or a movie. He would dawdle over an occasional beer—or a very long-lasting cup of coffee in the automat. Then, in the late afternoon he'd return home, just as if he'd been to his job.

This suited Becky—for it left her free to continue her own busy, active routines as housewife, club member, relative, and friend. Becky had her capable hand in lots of things. Many people enjoyed her warm, hearty company and counted on her kind help when it was needed. Of course, now her activity was curtailed by her stubbornly painful feet. She was able to go out less and less. She used the telephone more and more. But she still commanded her own life—firmly, loudly, and with humor.

That same evening, however, Bob was late. Becky waited nervously for him . . . her anxiety increasing as afternoon grew into dusk and then evening. There was nowhere to telephone. Nothing to do to ease the nagging fear in her breast. She sat at the window, looking down into the street.

The young policeman who knocked at the door made Becky feel very old indeed. He had brought Bob home. Bob, who had wandered for hours, having taken the wrong subway and lost his way. He'd been mugged, rolled, robbed, and ridiculed—and he staggered into Becky's arms weeping and cursing. The young policeman suggested politely that she not let him out alone anymore. "You better watch him, ma'am," he told her, "he might get hurt worse next time."

She calmed Bob, fed him, bathed him, and put him to bed like one of her babies. But there was no sleep that night for Becky. She lay awake thinking long and hard. If Bob couldn't find his way home here—what would happen to him if they ever moved to a new house?

No, Becky decided, as the first fingers of dawn pushed her into the next day, we're not moving from this house. Steps or no steps. Feet or no feet. If I have to be dragged up on a pulley, we will not move.

In vain Rita argued. In vain, she pointed out that if they would move to a housing project with an older adult center, Becky and Bob would both find friends . . . new things to do . . . Bob wouldn't feel he had to go "downtown" each day.

"Apply now," Rita implored. "You may have to wait a year to be placed."

But Becky had made her decision and nothing would change it.

Even though Bob became increasingly disoriented.

Even though her own legs sometimes refused to move another step. (Sometimes, when no one was looking, Becky would sit her huge bulk on the landing and gently slide down a few steps at a time—holding on to the railing —just to avoid standing on her feet.)

She was very careful to take excellent care of herself, for she knew Bob's life depended on her ability to function.

* * *

When Rita was called to the hospital, she found that Aunt Becky had broken a hip. Bob was devastated. Cousins and nieces rallied around to help care for him while Aunt Becky stayed in the hospital for the necessary surgery. When she was ready to be discharged, she wouldn't hear of going to a rehabilitation center. She took the walker, and went home to be with Bob. Rita never did know how she got up those three terrible flights of stairs. Subsequently, however, when she was summoned by the doctor for follow-up visits at the hospital clinic, the hospital social service department sent an ambulance with two men who would carry her down, and then up again.

She was indomitable. Day after day she sat in her living room, leaning on the walker, issuing clear demanding orders to her various helpers. She joked, she laughed, and she dictated.

Only at night, she wept. Wept and worried—for she knew Bob had cancer, and that she herself wasn't well. What would become of them?

Finally, her doctor told her that if she wanted to live and care for Bob, she better undergo serious internal surgery. That was when she reopened the discussion with Rita.

"What are my alternatives?" she asked. "I'm beginning to feel that I can't manage our lives anymore. And I can't watch over Bob. He's been losing his way . . . he's been mugged three times."

Rita hesitated. Things had become quite difficult by now. Family members, themselves with home problems, were traveling from all over the city to help. The Department of Social Service provided a part-time domestic worker . . . but there were thousands of additional small chores for which she had no time. Time was running out. It no longer seemed reasonable to apply to housing . . . a year, at this point, seemed too long to wait.

Yet, it's pretty tough to tell your favorite aunt, who had helped you with your own four babies . . . and shared your joys in their growing up . . . to apply to an institution.

Becky spared her. With a deep sigh, she asked, "How long do you think I'll have to wait if I apply to the home for the aged?"

Rita helped her with the forms, the telephone calls, the home visits from the caseworker. The process lasted several months. Finally, Mr. and Mrs. Brown received formal notice to report for an interview with Mr. Johnson, an admitting social worker, and for their physical and psychiatric examinations.

The Home for the Aged was a solid old building. It stood on a hilltop overlooking what had once been a pocket of quiet in the growing city, but was now the center of a noisy, crowded, very poor ghetto community. On this gloomy day, the building looked like a monolithic gray mass against the clouded sky. The indoor hallways were in tones of gray—unrelieved today, by a single ray of sunshine. The building was quiet. A few old people shuffled softly about in the lobby. White-coated staff members walked about briskly, laughing and chatting with each other, often in brittle rapid Spanish.

Rita, Becky, and Bob were greeted by Mr. Johnson and ushered into his tiny office. The interview went pleasantly. Mr. Johnson was gentle with Uncle Bob who, unthreatened, responded rather appropriately. When they went upstairs for the physical and psychiatric exams, Rita waited anxiously for them in the lounge. When Mr. Johnson returned to summon her, she knew by his look that they had hit a snag.

Back in the tiny office, the social worker turned to Aunt Becky. "Mrs. Brown," he said, "the doctors have certified you for immediate admission. We could have you here in residence within two weeks."

"And my husband?" Becky asked. "We are applying as a couple you know. We don't want to be separated. Can he be admitted just as soon?"

The social worker shook his head. "I'm sorry," he said. "The doctors will not admit him at all."

"But why?" she asked.

"He's too disoriented. Our facility is not equipped to cope with him," was his reply.

"But I'll take care of him," she implored. "I'll watch over him. I won't let him get in anybody's way."

"We can't permit that. You see, you are here to be taken care of yourself."

There was no recourse. The doctors had decided. Of course, Mr. Brown could be referred to a private nursing home . . . they would be glad to make a referral. . . .

Aunt Becky stood up in the middle of his speech. Leaning on her walker with one hand, gripping Uncle Bob's coat sleeve with the other, she said, "I'm sorry we took up your time, Mr. Johnson. Thank you, but no thanks."

Rita drove them both home and somehow managed to help them upstairs. Aunt Becky never said another word about the application, about moving, or about any other kind of change. She went back to her seat in the living room, back to the routine of giving orders to anyone who could be pressed into service. Only she smiled less. And laughed not at all. And the sunny beam had left her kindly face.

About six months later, Uncle Bob died after a short illness at home. When her mourning period was over, Aunt Becky picked up the telephone and called Mr. Johnson.

"My husband is dead now," she told him. Her voice was firm, unclouded by tears. "I can dispose of my household in about three weeks. How soon can you admit me to your institution?"

Shura Saul

The Vegetable

"Millie . . . Millie Talbert."

Who was calling from somewhere far, far away? And who was being called? The syllables were familiar . . . where had she heard that name?

She sank back into the pain. She knew this ever-present feeling must be pain, although she wasn't sure exactly where in her body it was, or why. But sometimes, mercifully, it would be eased. And when that happened, the energy it took to bear the pain would release . . . and she would realize, in the new comfort, that this old nagging feeling must be pain.

That voice—with its persistent calling—seemed to release the same energy within her. Her thoughts, usually amorphous and blanketed, began to shape themselves slowly into questions.

Where was she now?

And how long had she been there?

And who was this Millie they were calling?

Millie . . . the syllables echoed softly, persistently, through the sluggish crevices of her thoughts. There was a little girl once, and a white house, and a smiling mother. When the girl grew up, there was John—sweet and loving John. Like air and sunlight, he was always there. The little girl grew older . . . then he went away. Where? Where had John gone? Oh yes, he had died. And the old lady who had been the little girl was left all alone in an empty, empty house.

Then had come illness, and doctors and medicines and hospitals.

Faces always bending over her as she lay weakly in the bed, or huddled in the wheelchair swaddled in pillows to prop her and soften the hurt.

The firm voice of a man telling her not to worry . . . John had left her well provided . . . bills would be attended.

Loneliness and dreariness . . . strange faces and familiar pain.

Too much . . . too much to bear . . . until her mind had blotted it all out with a dark curtain of soft forgetfulness . . . closed her eyes to all the emptiness.

"Millie, . . . Millie Talbert, . . . open your eyes."

So far away that voice. She strained to catch the words.

Now hands were pushing gently at her, rocking her supine body, intruding. . . .

What did it want, that voice? Why was it prodding at her? Where were her eyes?

Of course she did have eyes. She thought very hard—trying to remember her where—in this massive burden of her body—her eyes could be. Her mind pushed and tugged at the lids . . . a sharp new pain pierced her head as she worked.

"You are only fluttering your eyelids," the voice said—still faint and distant—but commanding. "Can't you do better than that?"

No. No she couldn't. The silent negative stabbed her weariness. No. It was too hard. She stopped her efforts. She didn't want to try so hard anymore.

"You don't answer," the voice said with some disappointment. "Why don't you answer me? I know you can talk."

But I have answered—she said silently—how is it that you didn't hear my answer?

"Are you thirsty?" the gentle voice asked again. "Would you like a drink?"

She must have nodded . . . because the familiar drinking straw was in her mouth now—and the cool, sweet liquid trickled down her throat . . . pleasant . . . easy . . . comforting.

"Now, open your eyes," the voice insisted . . . pleased. "I know you hear me. You nodded when you wanted the drink."

She tried again. This time she worked very-very hard. How tired it was making her!

The voice came closer and whispered. "I can see how hard you are trying. I'll come back tomorrow. Perhaps if you try a little, every day, you will do it. . . .

"Then you will see my face. You will see this bright lovely room. You will see the smiles around . . . and beautiful flowers. But first, you must open your eyes. Then you will know where you are."

Where? Where was she? Who was she?

The voice went on kindly, "Goodbye for today. Goodbye Millie . . . Millie Talbert."

Ah yes, it was herself. She was Millie Talbert. This pool of pain, this twisted body was herself . . . Millie.

That was enough for this day. She swam back into her emptiness, exhausted. The voice had vanished. There were only hands at her body now . . . hurting . . . then soothing. A sharp sting in some part of her—and then forgetfulness again.

Shura Saul

Old People Talk About Death

The scene is the thirtieth session of a mental health group led by a trained psychotherapist in a nursing home. The group consists of five women, their ages ranging from 75 to 88 years. They are all ambulatory and alert; each suffering from a physical ailment requiring some level of nursing care. Within a range of capacity for ego functioning, each of them is related to reality and is competent in some decision making concerning her immediate needs and problems.

This group experience is part of an interdisciplinary treatment program that is consciously aimed at keeping these women reality oriented through such problem solving and decision making as may be possible within the severely circumscribed circumstances, physical and emotional, of the nursing home setting.

The psychotherapist had recently returned from a trip to England, which he had discussed with the group the preceeding week. Among other things, he had reported that many small towns now use crematoria instead of cemeteries. This had occasioned interest in the question of burial versus cremation, and the group had decided to pursue the subject at its next session. During the week between the two sessions, there had been two deaths of some significance to these women. A resident had died, and also the sister of another resident.

The psychotherapist has had to deal with depression, a continuous condition of residents in an institution. Knowing of their suppressed fear of death, and their repression of feelings about the death of others, the therapist felt that it would be valuable to offer an opportunity for expressing these feelings through a discussion like this one.

The five group members include:

Mrs. Howard. A very bright, alert woman of 75, active in all phases of the nursing home program.

Mrs. Rose. A smiling, well-dressed woman who usually denies problems; was friendly with Mrs. Robbins before coming to this home.

Mrs. Robbins. A calm, alert woman who had been Mrs. Rose's neighbor when they both lived in the community.

Mrs. Riker. A tall, angular woman with a deep voice and quick laughter.

Mrs. Moran. A soft-voice, quiet, visually handicapped woman who functions well and always dresses up for this meeting.

As usual, after the initial greetings, the discussion begins very slowly.

Dr. S. Do you remember what we said we'd be talking about this week?

Mrs. Howard. I remember, but it's better to talk about life, not about death.

Mrs. Rose. Talking about dying is a sad thing.

Dr. S. Do you think we shouldn't talk about it?

Mrs. Rose. I realize you can't bring the dead back. . . . it depends how you talk about them.

Dr. S. Remember, last week we planned to talk about burial or cremation?

Mrs. Robbins. She (pointing to Mrs. Rose) had her husband cremated. Do you remember that? (She turns to Mrs. Rose)

Mrs. Rose. That is right. That was how he wished it.

Dr. S. What do you think about it?

Mrs. Rose. Well, if it happened to me, I'd just as soon go that way.

Dr. S. So your wish is to be cremated?

Mrs. Rose. Yes!

Dr. S. How do the rest of you feel?

Mrs. Robbins. I'm Catholic. I don't believe in cremation.

Dr. S. How about you, Mrs. Moran?

Mrs. Moran. I don't like to hear that story.

Dr. S. What story?

Mrs. Moran. I want to be buried just like my husband . . . my father (Very softly).

Mrs. Riker. (Very matter of fact) I wonder how much it costs to be cremated. It must be cheaper, I'm sure.

Dr. S. That's not why they do it in England. It's because there, they have no space.

Mrs. Riker. Since Peggy (Mrs. Rose) has had experience, maybe she will tell us more about it (cremation), some little thing.

Mrs. Rose. (Schoolteacher style) You should go to such a funeral, then you'll know more about it.

Dr. S. I think Mrs. Riker wants to know your experience.

Mrs. Rose. Well, it was my husband's wish . . . he always said when it happened to him, . . . that's why I had it done. That's how I felt at the time, and you can imagine that yourself.

Mrs. Robbins. They had a wake the night before the cremation.

Dr. S. How did you feel about it?

Mrs. Robbins. I didn't mind. When you're dead, you're dead.

Dr. S. What would you want for yourself?

Mrs. Robbins. No, I don't want it. I want to be buried with my husband and my family.

Dr. S. Do you think there is a hereafter?

Mrs. Robbins. Yes, you have to account for your sins, . . . and then you will get together.

Dr. S. Then you have a religious reason for preferring burial?

Mrs. Robbins. Yes, that's right.

Dr. S. Mrs. Moran, what about you?

Mrs. Moran. Me? Poor, blind me?

Dr. S. What would you want?

Mrs. Moran. I want my sight back—if I can have what I want.

Dr. S. What about cremation or burial?

Mrs. Moran. All I want is to be buried with my husband, my friends, and my people. I want to be with the people I love so much, and with the baby that died, too.

Dr. S. So you, too, believe in a hereafter?

Mrs. Moran. That is right.

Dr. S. Mrs. Riker?

Mrs. Riker. Oh, it wouldn't make any difference to me. I think I'm going to be buried. A lot of people think that the worms won't eat you if you're not buried. Some people think they'll hate to lie there—the worms will eat them. It makes no difference to me. Whatever goes on after I'm gone, I won't know anyway! They can throw me over the fence and I'll lay there and I can rot there. It won't make any difference!
(She laughs. . . . there is general laughter . . . aud some relief)

Dr. S. Well, we finally got a laugh out of this. Mrs. Howard, how about you?

Mrs. Howard. I'd like to be buried where my husband is.

Dr. S. So, you want to be buried too?

Mrs. Howard. I have a plot there. (She is suddenly thoughtful). . . . I have the deed . . . but I didn't pay my dues . . . I don't know what I should do now . . . if they are very scarce with the plots (Suddenly defiant) . . . I don't care. Whatever the children want!

Dr. S. Whatever your children want?

Mrs. Howard. I gave them the deed to the plot.

Dr. S. So you want to be buried?

Mrs. Howard. I don't know what I want. (Sadly) I suppose so.

Dr. S. Any particular reason?

Mrs. Howard. (Very softly) No reason . . . no particular reason . . . I belonged to a society . . . where I got the plot and then I couldn't pay dues . . . I paid a little, then I stopped. Maybe I lost the plot because of "off-payment."

Dr. S.   Well, we could find out for you, if you wish.

Mrs. Howard.   Yes, I would want you to do that.

Dr. S.   Do you ladies think about death?

Mrs. Robbins.   Yes, I think of it . . . sure!

Mrs. Moran.   By golly, I do! I wish it very bad sometimes!

Dr. S.   Mrs. Riker, how about you?

Mrs. Riker.   I don't so much now, as when I was a kid. When you're a child, you are afraid of death. But now, when you know it is coming, you can't stop it.

Mrs. Robbins.   I'm not thinking about it, because I don't want to go there.

Mrs. Riker.   Where?

Mrs. Robbins.   To the—uh—crematorium.

Mrs. Moran.   (Her voice suddenly pitched high) I think of it, off and on, I speak with my daughters.

Dr. S.   Are you frightened by it?

Mrs. Moran.   (Soft voice again) No, I'm not frightened.

Mrs. Robbins.   Sometimes I just wonder what will happen to me after I die.

Dr. S.   Does anyone else think of that?

Mrs. Rose.   Sometimes I just hope that they'll put me where I want to go, that's all. I want to be cremated.

Mrs. Robbins.   She wants to be with her husband.
(There is a long silence)

Dr. S.   Did you leave any papers to that effect? Any message with anyone?

Mrs. Rose.   Oh yes, to the people who are concerned.

Dr. S.   How many of you have made arrangements for burial?
(There is another long silence)

Mrs. Riker.   I have a grave from my husband's insurance.
(Suddenly there is an active hubbub among the ladies . . . they have begun small buzzing conversations between themselves . . . finally Mrs. Robbins turns to Dr. S.)

Mrs. Robbins.   I just say I'm old, and they'll have to bury me.

Mrs. Howard.   Don't they have plans here in the nursing home?

Dr. S.   Why, do you think I'm selling plots?
(There is general laughter which relieves the tension)

Mrs. Riker.   It feels good to laugh . . . we all needed that laugh.

Dr. S.   Does this whole discussion disturb you?

Mrs. Riker.   No, not me.

Mrs. Howard.   Now, I have the occasion to ask, why such a discussion? Why did it come up here?

Dr. S.   Well, did anything happen in the home here this past week involving someone who died?
(Silence)

Mrs. Howard.   Yes. Rose, Mrs. Ellis's sister, she died. I wanted to go to the funeral, but then I made another plan and I stayed away.

Dr. S.   *I* think Mrs. Moran doesn't know what you are talking about. Would you like to tell her?

Mrs. Howard.   (Suddenly overtly hostile) She doesn't know what I'm talking about, so she's gonna be without it.

Dr. S.   Who died?

Mrs. Howard.   The sister died. Mrs. Ellis' sister.

Mrs. Robbins.   (Interrupts suddenly) Mrs. Leland died.
(Nobody pays any attention to her at this point)

Dr. S.   Is this news to anybody? About Mrs. Ellis' sister?

Mrs. Howard.   A few people from this place went to the funeral with Mrs. Ellis, that's all. I wasn't there.

Dr. S.   Who else, did you say, died this week, Mrs. Robbins?

Mrs. Robbins.   Mrs. Leland.
(There is another buzzing of interest over this bit of information, above which emerges the slightly Irish brogue of Mrs. Moran)

Mrs. Moran.   Oh, did she die?

Mrs. Robbins.   Yes, she did.

Mrs. Moran.   I didn't know she died.

Mrs. Robbins.   She was sick a long time.

Mrs. Moran.   (Incredulous) The lady on my floor? That Mrs. Leland?

Dr. S.   Yes. Does that upset you, Mrs. Moran?

Mrs. Moran.   (Amazed) They took such good care of her!

Mrs. Riker.   She was supposed to be very wealthy . . . many years ago. Mrs. Leland, one of the Leland dress house family.

Mrs. Howard.   Money doesn't pay off the death. Money doesn't pay off not to die.

Dr. S.   Um . . . um. . . .
(There is a deep, long silence)
Well, if I'm quiet will everyone else be quiet too?

Mrs. Howard.   (Sarcastically) Maybe somebody should start dancing. Mrs. Moran should play the music, then we wouldn't be so quiet.

Dr. S. You want us to play some music and everybody dance?

Mrs. Howard. (Softer tone) They won't dance. I'm just joking.

Dr. S. You're angry with me, Mrs. Howard?

Mrs. Howard. Because you picked such a topic today . . . we got to have a little bit of fun.

Dr. S. I have upset you.

Mrs. Howard. Of course, the topic upset me! It doesn't make me happy. It doesn't make me sad.

Dr. S. Shall we stop the discussion now? I'm asking everyone.

Mrs. Riker. (With a laugh) You're the boss.
(There are murmurs of general concensus)

Mrs. Howard. (Pleased voice) Well, let's ask the group to do the memory exercises. Let's see if we know the names of the people here, the live ones. . . .

The group accedes and begins their weekly name game to exercise their memory faculties.

NOTE: Two weeks after this discussion, Mrs. Rose died suddenly. She was cremated as was her wish. In the session that followed her death, the group members talked freely with each other and with the therapist about their feelings at her sudden passing.

In sharp contrast to earlier situations when such feelings had been repressed, and conversations had ignored the fact of death, Mrs. Riker opened the session by asking the therapist, "Do you notice that someone is missing from our group?"

Young People Talk About Death

The scene is a recreation room in a summer camp in upstate New York. The teenage girl campers (ages 14 to 16) are participants in a work program. Most of them have been friendly visitors and recreation aides in a local nursing home. A few have been assisting at a center for cerebral palsied youth in another nearby facility. The following discussion contains verbatim excerpts from tapes of a seminar; one of several held during the summer as interpretative accompaniments to these girls' fieldwork experiences.

Rita.   Well, I work in the old age home and most of the time we talk to people, and . . . uh . . . there was this man that died two days ago, that I became very close with. And he was blind. He never really talked to anybody, but I fed him. Then I was sick for two days on the day that I left . . . on Saturday, he was fine and everything was all right. The next few days, he got very sick and Wednesday he died. It was a shock to me and I really missed him. I still miss him now. They've got a new guy in his bed, he must . . . (she gulps a little and trips over the words) he was just like a part of me. I missed him a lot and I still do but I feel that he was 80 years old and he lived a long life and everything was all right and (Fumbles . . . the words are unclear) that was as much as he could expect . . . and so there wasn't anything I could do about it.

Leader.   How many of you have already had similar experiences? (There is a buzz of voices . . . above which rises the high pitched tones saying)

Bobbie.   . . . I was feeding a man and he was about 80 and, like, I never really got close to him, but his condition was serious and I was glad when he died because he was really sick. He was in a coma and he really looked like he was in a lot of agony and everything . . . like he was suffering a lot.

Jennie.   I find it doesn't depress me at all and I find that the death bed doesn't faze me as much, 'cause many of them are just vegetables, so I think it is good that they die.

Leader.   (To Rita) You didn't feel like that, though, did you with this man?

Rita.   No.

Leader.   What is the difference?

Rita.   Because I'd become close to him, and like, I knew him. And it makes a difference. Because there are a lot of other people there that none of the other girls are close with, and if it would happen to them, I guess they'd have the same feeling as Jennie.

Leader.   What was the essential difference between your having been close to this man, and some of the experiences the others here may be having?

Rita.   Well, the difference is, the people . . . the people we are and the people they are. I related to him more than someone else might, and the empathy we had was different.

Leader.   You had something going between you that Bobbie, here, didn't seem to have with the man she was feeding. You had a relationship with him . . . it was the human quality of person-to-person that made the difference—isn't that so? Are some of you finding this to be true—either with older people or the cerebral palsy program?

Carol.   Yes. I've been working at the CP Center. It's not bad . . . there was one boy there, Larry . . . like I didn't really get very close to him but I

have some sort of special contact with him. I was able to talk to him and
he was able to talk to me. And like, if something ever happened to him
—like if he got sick or something I guess I would feel the way Rita
felt. It would be a shock. I wouldn't expect it at all. He's younger—
though—not old like this other man was.

Ann. It's really funny. Lenny, our supervisor told us that it would be possible that some we'd be working with might die. I saw it in the hospital.
There was this old lady, about 85 or 86—and like, she was fine. She was
eating—like she was hoping to get out of the hospital. And then, she
started to get worse. Like she realized there was nothing to live for. She
stopped eating and she began to complain. It got to the point where people didn't pay any attention to her. When I got to her, I felt like I was
acting towards her just like everyone else was . . . like once she was a
person that wanted to share with people and talk to them. But then, it
got out of hand and all she did was complain. That's all I knew her as. I
was kind of prepared for it—like Lenny told us it might happen . . .
and, as Rita said—more than one person died in the hospital. We have
to be prepared for it . . . a lot of us are going to be experiencing it.

Leader. If you listen to what Ann just said, you'd realize that you are not
really talking about dying and death. What are we talking about? Ann,
what did you just say about this old lady?

Ann. I was talking about the experiences I had with her before she died
. . . what she had been like and what she turned into.

Leader. You see, we are really talking about living and being alive. When I
asked Rita what was the difference between her experiences and Bobby's,
she talked about the quality of a living relationship with that blind man.
It is this quality of life that is the essence of our activity with people.
Even when we are talking about dying. Does that seem fantastic to you?
Because, being alive ourselves, we can only think of death in terms of
life . . . that's all we, as human beings really *know* about. And so, when
we talk about death, we talk of it as an act of *not living* . . . if we can
address that quality of life, we begin to get to the heart of what we need
to understand in our dealings with people . . . even when they are
dying. What does that bring to mind?

Rita. What she used to be . . . like someone that was a person who could
help herself. But she also needed help from others. But, when she died it
was like she had not really been living any more before that. She refused
to help herself. She was not working with herself. She was working
against herself.

Bobby. What was wrong with her?

Ann. I think she was just old. Or maybe she even talked herself into being
sick. Because she said, "It's natural that I lived my life and right now

. . . I just don't feel like eating today." It got to the point where she was very weak. It was like she was saying, "Well, I'm not ready for my time to come, . . ." she was just fighting against herself.

Bobby. I don't think there is anything wrong with that. If she feels that she has lived her life . . . if she feels maybe now she should stop.

Rita. We're talking about what was . . . what life is. Life is living it with a feeling of brotherhood . . . with a purpose. And, like, for knowing what death is—we really don't know. You know what I mean?

Carol. Maybe that's how she saw it. Maybe she really had enough and wanted to die. For her, living like she was living was death.

Mary. (In a quiet, disturbed voice . . . she hadn't spoken until now.) Maybe I could say that too, right now. I could say, my life is over, I really have nothing to live for. But maybe it's not right . . . that's no reason to die . . . maybe it's because I'm young now that I look at it this way. When I get old, will I really feel that too? Like there is nobody left. Like there is nothing left to do—so there is nobody and nothing left for me. I'm liable to get that way when I get older.

So Live!

With trembling fingers, she opened her worn bag and fumbled for the key. Her heart beat wildly as she inserted it into the lock and opened the door. Four months . . . four long agonizing months of fighting illness and anger and loneliness and pain . . . of fighting death itself in that hospital . . . not knowing when, if ever, she would return to this little one-room apartment.

The autumn sunlight smiled a warm welcome through the dusty windows. She hung her old coat into the closet and looked around the room. She had left it neat, even though she'd been so sick and she could hardly move her hands. The bed was made . . . the hand-embroidered throw pillows nicely arranged. The sink was clear of dishes. The little wet spot on the ceiling seemed somewhat larger than she remembered. Apparently the landlord hadn't yet fixed the upstairs leak. It was good to be home.

She sat down to rest. She hadn't realized how tiring it would be, just making the trip from the hospital. How weak she was feeling now! For a moment she panicked. Maybe all the people in the hospital had been right after all—pressuring and discouraging her when her discharge was being arranged. Was she really going to be able to take care of herself at home?

With a sigh, she went into the bathroom to wash up and to look into the mirror. She knew there was no answer to the question without first dealing with the image she would behold. As before, she flinched at the sight as she forced herself to look. Was this disfigured apparition really herself, Fanny Blackman?

What a bad job they had done with her face! Before the surgery she had been—well—not bad-looking. Almost pretty. She had been a bit vain about her tiny upturned nose, small mouth, delicate high cheekbones. How could she ever accept as her own—this distorted face which had been somehow anatomically disarranged?

Her features looked as if some child had cut a picture from a magazine, folded and torn it in half, and then had repasted it clumsily and inaccurately. The entire left side seemed to belong to the "other side" of the fold. The left eyelid hung drunkenly over the dull brown eye . . . that would never see again. The left side of the mouth drooped—upper lip flapped slightly over the lower as if a cigarette were to be hung permanently within the fold. The nose was too large, and also lopsided . . . the left nostril flaring slightly.

She had asked the doctor why they couldn't have shaped it more like her own. He had tried to explain, but she had been too sick, really, to hear him. All she remembered now was that he said they had done "the best they could."

He had been quite frank with her. "You've been very sick, Miss Blackman," he had said. But she noticed that he wasn't looking directly into her eyes. She hated that—when people didn't look straight at you as they talked. She had always felt they must be lying, or insincere. Now, as the doctor's eyes turned away from her face, she realized that maybe he just couldn't bear to look at it! And in the same instant, she understood how differently she would have to view others from now on—because of how she herself looked at them. She'd have to forgive people for not looking at her, for example, just as she was, this moment, forgiving the doctor. And she wouldn't be able to judge sincerity this way, either!

The doctor had been quite nice though. "We think we caught it all," he said. "We did a lot of surgery, you know, and grafting. Your vision and your hearing have both been affected. You'll probably need a hearing aid a little later on—but right now, the thing to do is give yourself a chance to get well . . . rest . . . eat properly. You'll be all right for a while."

Recalling that session now as she confronted herself in the mirror, her right eye filled with tears. She fought them back. At least the white hair above the tormented face was the same as ever. The curls were disheveled . . . she needed a shampoo and set. Her blue dress hung big, too big, on her tiny frame. She had lost weight in the hospital.

She pushed the mirrored door aside to open the medicine chest behind it . . . partly to efface her bizarre image . . . partly to—what? There on the shelf, tantalizingly, stood the bottle of pills, the very ones she had handled with indecision four months ago to the day.

She put out her hand, picked up the bottle, and began a dialogue—partly with herself, partly with the pills. "So you're back, Fanny! Well, you see, we are still here, still waiting for you. Will you spurn us again, Fanny? You look a lot worse now than you did when you left us. Maybe we look better to you now, eh?"

"I took a chance," she said. "I wanted to live."

"So—you lived. . . ." The pills taunted her. "So here you are—alive! Frail, and weak, and all alone in the world—with that horror of a face. How are you going to live now, Fanny Blackman?'

How will you live? That's what they had all asked her, there at the hospital. It hadn't really been a question at all. Everyone who asked it seemed to have his own answer for her, different from her answer, it seemed.

The young social worker had come—after surgery—asking about her plans. Plans? Fanny had stared at her. "I'm going home."

Well, it seemed that the young worker had thought perhaps Fanny wouldn't be able to live at home anymore. Maybe, she suggested gently, Fanny would like to consider a change in her living arrangements? Nursing home, perhaps? Some other type of institution?

Fanny was shocked! But then, she realized, the social worker didn't know about her sunny little apartment, the soft pastel-colored Renoir prints, the carved old rocker by the window. Fanny had tried to tell her—but the social worker kept asking how was she going "to manage"—and hadn't seemed to understand about the apartment at all.

Some of the nurses, too, in their kind (but blind) way said similar things. "You're going to need someone to look after you, poor dear. What will you do in the lonely winter? And who will take care of you when you get sick?"

Even her one and only friend Betty, when she came to visit all the way from Yonkers where she lived now, worried out loud how Fanny would ever again manage alone in Flushing, with no close friends nearby to help her.

"It isn't as if you'll be able to run around, go out to the movies and things," Betty said. "You'll be cooped up by yourself all the time, especially in the winter."

As they all clucked their tongues and worried about her, Fanny had wondered herself. She knew better than they what it was like to be all alone and sick. She had learned some tricks of survival in the city jungle. She remembered how hard it had been, at first, to get groceries delivered. Supermarkets couldn't be bothered. You couldn't even get their phone numbers from information! Finally, she had found a small store whose prices were higher. But the old man who owned it had a name, and a telephone number, and a grandson named Joey who delivered. She always give Joey a tip. A new thought slid quickly into her mind. Would he be willing to deliver now, once he saw her new face? Would she have to make the tip larger? She could hardly afford that. . . .

Yes, yes. There were ways to beat the jungle, even in this unfriendly city. It was too bad she hadn't had a chance to make friends with her neighbors before she became ill. Now, she wasn't even going to try. Who'd want to be friendly with this new face of hers? She'd always think they were pitying her. That was one thing she couldn't tolerate.

She reached for the bottle of pills. Held them in her hand.

"Well, what now," they mocked her.

That question, too, was one she'd been answering for months. One decision after another—which doctor, which hospital, which treatment. Finally —when she had been told about the radical surgery, she had stood here, just like this, with the same bottle in her hand. But it had been a different Fanny Blackman who had looked into that mirror—weighing the certainty of the slim bottle against the unknown terrors that lay ahead. She had talked aloud to herself then, to break the blanket of silence around her—to hear as well as to think her thoughts.

"Fanny. You are 72 years old and all alone in the world. You are sick with cancer . . . and who knows what you'll be like if you go through with this operation. Take the pills, maybe, and be done with it. It's enough."

But she hadn't taken the pills. She shook them angrily now. "Well, now I know what I'm like after the operation. I certainly didn't want a face like this. It wasn't so much that I wanted to live . . . but I suppose I just didn't want to die then."

"And now, Fanny," the pills retorted silently. "What now?"

Fanny felt the answer shaping itself somewhere deep in herself—like a twisting tornado it corkscrewed through her body in one silent sound—HELP!

Deep within her, the word had been an angry scream, a raging volcano. But as it pushed its way out through her twisted lips, it sounded to her ears like a whispered prayer.

And Fanny heard it as her own answer. "Help is for living."

She replaced the bottle. "Stay there," she said to the pills. "Maybe someday I'll come back to you. Not now."

She closed the mirror-door firmly and looked at the ugly stranger who had moved into her life. Again she spoke aloud.

"So, my dear, you are Fanny Blackman. Some beauty you are, Fanny, it took you a lifetime to become such a beauty.

"Well, it's the same question, my friend. And you keep on finding the same answer, it seems. You wanted to live, Fanny? You came home to live? So now—live!"

She turned to the closet, put on her coat, placed her patched old shopping bag on her arm, locked the door, and walked into the golden sunlight of the autumn afternoon to do her marketing.

Shura Saul

Love, Loneliness and Loss

What time is it?
What day?
What season of the year?
I am the child seeking mother
Or no—
I was the mother
Now the child is gone.

Where are they all
With whom, for whom I live
or lived?
For whom I cared and care—

Who cares for me?

An alien face appears,
Strange hands place food upon my dish
And somehow minister to my needs
Til early evening ends.
As shades
Linger into long and lonely night
The day, and alien face, both fade.

My mirror mocks my frightened face—
Panicked eyes in empty space
Seeking them, the active ones
Who filled my life—each day.
And who am I, and where,
What time, what year is this
Anyway?

Shura Saul

Letters of Two Men

By Themselves

February 10
Santa Monica, California

Dear Avrom,

I am writing to you on this, the first anniversary of Judith's death . . . my dear sister and your beloved wife. Though we live a continent apart, we are close to each other through our love for her. I can never forget how you took care of her during her illness —pushing her wheelchair to the hospital and back. I have kept her letters and yours—I have read them over and over . . . to remember how fortunate she was to have you as a husband . . . you, who did everything possible to make her life easier during the last long months of her illness. Your relationship as husband and wife are beautifully described in your letters—and I, far away from you both, am grateful for the way you shared it all with me.

We are two old men—without our wives. Your letters to me are always a source of pleasure . . . and a reminder of our long standing friendship . . . for this, as for other things . . . I shall never forget my sister.

Sincerely,

Sam

February 20
New York City

My dear brother Sam,

Your letter touched a vulnerable spot in my heart . . . that is, our Judith. In our society (which I see as quite swampy politically, economically and morally), it is often frowned upon to express one's sentiments. I ask, why should that be? Is not a person entitled to express his thoughts and feelings? Is not every day of one's life a holiday . . . a day of joy, or sometimes grief . . . but yet a holiday? I believe that no person has the right to insult another. . . . to make him feel bad. But how does society dare to oppress an individual's feelings . . . shame him from expressing his happiness or suffering?

Judith is very much alive in my memory. A picture of our little family hangs over my desk . . . both of us, much younger . . . and little Sarah. Now Sarah has grown children . . . how the years fly! Judith's name is often spoken, not only in my house, but in Sarah's house, and in the homes of our mutual friends. It is no accident that we speak of her . . . for in her lifetime she earned the love of so many through the way she lived her own life, through her relationships with people, her kind deeds, her sweet and friendly face, her beautiful eyes . . . her susceptible heart.

You know, dear Sam, I am not a hypocrite. I am a plain honest man who likes to speak as he thinks. I do not write you these things because you are her brother . . . but because they are true. She and I were a real team. This was so, not because we both came from the same small town in Russia . . . not because our parents prayed in the same small synagogue; not because your father, who was the town miller, bought hardware from my father's store back there in the Ukraine; but because we just seemed to fit together. I remember, the first week after we were married, you wrote her a letter asking how it felt to live far away from her family, with a stranger like me! Her answer to you warmed my heart . . . I felt so much a man when I read it, for she wrote, "Even though I've lived with him only one week, I feel as if I've known him all my life!"

Those were her feelings toward me, and mine toward her . . . even though this was my second marriage, and I already had my little child. She helped me bring up my daughter . . . for this alone, I should adore her. She fitted in with my own family . . . and she tactfully and beautifully helped me remain friends with Sarah's mother's family.

You speak of my pushing the wheelchair. Who else should have done that? She was my wife, my comrade, my flesh and blood. She was so sick, then, it tore the heart out of me. And, to top it off, I had to perform a daily injection into her thigh . . . not with a thin needle but with one as thick as the tooth of a fork because the liquid itself was so thick it couldn't pass through a small lumen. Her thigh was so perforated from these daily injections, it looked like a sieve. I used to curse myself whenever I did it, but she had to have it every day, or else she would die. One might almost think this was a punishment from heaven (why upon me?) to inflict needles into the body of my best friend, my beloved wife.

Even as I write to you, my hands shiver with the memory.

People like her are a rarity. How she respected you and your father. How she worried over her younger brothers. And to the youngest, Jacob, she was like a mother! When your sister Ninotchka fell ill, she traveled, sick herself, to Chicago, hoping to persuade her to change her ways. And, finally, when Nina had to be brought to New York from Chicago, how Judith embraced me when I said I would go fetch her! When your father was ill, Judith cared for him . . . she was the only one who could make him comfortable . . . and would sit up in a chair all night watching him.

Was there, then, a limit to her gallantry? I am a poor writer, and cannot describe the treasures of this human soul. You knew her as a sister, a young kid, a schoolgirl, and a young lady. I knew her as a grown up person, a woman, wife and mother. As a housewife . . . member of her community. As a friend to others.

When she became ill, she never complained. To all her visitors, at home or in the hospital, she would say, "How are you? Tell me about yourself."

I would have pushed that wheelchair from here to California. Now she is gone. I have no guilt before anyone to speak of her. She was the brightest element in one important epoch of my life. A beautiful memory, which I cherish along with others.

Thank you for your note, dear Sam. Let us write often.

Avrom

Coming Home

Carol P. Saul

It was the first Sunday of my vacation. My mother and I were relaxing over a second cup of coffee chatting comfortably the way we used to before I went away to college. My mother set her coffee cup down and said, "Debbie, Dad and I are going to see Gram today." I didn't look up, and she hesitated. "I realize you don't get a chance to come home very often and I hate to ask anything of you when you're here, but—will you come with us?"

What she meant was that I had to go. After all, I was Gram's favorite granddaughter, and I hadn't seen her in more than six months, ever since her stroke. Of course I loved Gram, and visiting her had always been more of a pleasure than an obligation, but the truth was that I was afraid to see her changed. Mom had written me how Gram had fallen down the stairs when she had the stroke and how her children had decided that letting her live alone was too risky. While she was recovering in the hospital, Mom and my uncles sold the big old house that Gram had maintained so long for herself and reserved a place for her in one of the better, or so they had been assured, nursing homes. Mom took her to stay at our house for awhile after the hospital had discharged her, and then Gram had gone to live at the Home.

"Debbie?" My mother was waiting for an answer.

"Oh, I'll go," I said and, afraid that my answer had sounded too grudging, I added hastily, "It's not that I don't want to see Gram or anything, it's just that I—that I—."

"I know, Deb," my mother said gently, and a look of pain came into her soft brown eyes. "But I know she'd love to see you again. Your uncles don't even want to make the effort to visit." Her voice was bitter. "Last week I told her that Eddie and Joe would be up to see her soon, and she looked at me with that new blank expression and asked me who Joe and Eddie were." She pursed her lips. "I keep telling her every week that she has two sons, but they never come to see her. It's no wonder she forgets." She stared past me out the kitchen window. "She's gotten so old, so fast."

That chilled me. I was used to thinking about Gram as a strong, active, fiercely independent woman, with white hair combed neatly back into a nape bun, moving briskly about her house in a homemade apron. Gram cooked and baked and put up preserves from the berries in her garden. She let no one help her with the housework, yet the house always looked as if she had just gone over it with her ancient carpet sweeper, no matter when we popped in for a visit. And she still had time to fix huge family dinners for as many as could squeeze into her dining room.

"Has she changed much, Mom?" I asked.

"Oh, Deb!" she exclaimed softly. "If you saw her now, you'd never guess how tall and straight she used to be. She never goes for walks anymore because there's no one at the Home to take her. And she's not getting the care that she should, or anything." She shook her head. "And for what we're paying, too," she added.

"But it's Gram's money, isn't it?'

"Oh, sure, its Gram's money." She pushed her cup and saucer away. "It's two lifetimes' worth of work, and at this rate it will be gone in five years. And she's not getting any pleasure out of it at all—remember how she and Grampa were going to use it to grow grapefruits?"

I nodded. The whole family always joked about the Florida citrus farm that Gram and Gramps would buy once they retired.

I reached across the table for Mom's cup and saucer and brought them to the sink. Above the rush of hot water I asked carefully, "Then why didn't you or Uncle Ed or Uncle Joe take Gram to live with you?"

There was a silence and my mother sighed. "It was the first thing we talked about, Deb. It just wouldn't work out. Ed has no room for her, you know that, with his five kids, and both Joe and Marian have their jobs. And the only time we have extra room is when you're at school. Besides I'd have to stay home with Gram all day. Really, Deb, it's much better for everyone concerned to have Gram in the Home." She got up decisively from the table and glanced at the new wall clock. "Daddy and Jimmy will be back soon. We'll have lunch and clean up, and we ought to be ready to leave about two."

She looked at me and her face softened. "Try not to be too shocked, Deb," she said. "Just be prepared."

My father and Jimmy came home shortly afterward. They carried on most of the conversation over lunch; I said little and ate less. When we had finished, my mother asked Jimmy if he was coming with us to see Gram. "Aw," he mumbled and wriggled in his chair. "You don't have to if you don't want to, son," Dad told him gently and with relief Jimmy said, "Okay, then I won't go," and ran off to his room. My parents exchanged glances.

"He goes more than any other grandchild," my father apologized.

"I know, Daddy," I said irritably. "I already told Mom I'd go."

"It's just that it's very hard for him," he began.

"I know, Daddy, I know!" I interrupted, a little angrily. I had heard it once; I was prepared now. They were building it up and at the same time trying to cushion me. It was almost as if they were trying to tell me about death for the first time, but they were afraid I'd cry. "Don't make such a big thing out of it, will you?" I got up from the table and started gathering up the plates. "It's all right, Deb," my mother said, half-rising from her chair. "I'll do the dishes."

"Sit down," I told her brusquely. "I'll do them." I threw the silver into the sink and turned the water on full force. Mom and dad looked at each other and left the kitchen.

On the way to the Home, my parents talked quietly and I huddled in the back seat staring out the window at the bare trees. Gram's house had been surrounded by tall oaks, trees that Grampa had planted himself when they first brought the house. And there had been two gardens. A flower garden in front and a kitchen garden—Gram's pride and joy—in the back. Who, I thought glumly, owned the house now? They wouldn't bother with all the wonderful growing things; the plants and cuttings would probably wither and die from neglect.

My father pulled into a half-empty parking lot beside the sprawling red brick building. A huge plate glass window reflected the neatly clipped lawn, brown and dead now. "Wilmot Nursing Home" proclaimed a big black and gold sign. By now the pale winter sun had warmed the air to an exhilarating briskness, but no one was sitting in the lawnchairs or walking on the cement pathway to take advantage of the break in the weather. I nudged my father.

"It's so nice out," I said. "Why don't they bring the stronger ones outside?"

My father shook his head. "It's probably too difficult to move them, Deb. And anyway, they don't have enough attendants to take care of the patients inside." We had unconsciously lowered our voices, as if we were entering a hospital or a funeral home or some other place where old age and death continually hover.

Dad held open the glass doors for us. I peered down the wide corridor, feeling uncomfortable. My father steered me forward and to the right. "Look, Deb, the recreaction room."

The smell of the place was so strong that I stepped back, trying to fight it off. It was a sickish sweetish conglomeration of aging flesh, urine, pine disinfectant, and the lingering perfume of visitors who had left long ago. I wanted to run. I longed for the fresh air outside and gripped my father's arm. "The smell," I whispered fiercely. He nodded, his nostrils drawn up. "I know. We've been coming here for months, and I still feel sick whenever that stink hits me."

We stood for a moment looking at the recreation room. Glass framed prints dotted the pale walls at precise intervals and, beneath them, the dull-faced residents sat in folding chairs. A few of them chatted together. Several of them looked up hungrily at us, and one old lady in a wheelchair beckoned to me with a clawlike hand. Two bored attendants exchanged laconic comments, and a nurse in a starched white cap wiped the face of a sweating, palsied old man. A few old people had visitors and, jealously guarding them in inescapable clusters of chairs, they leaned forward to grab onto every word. The visitors looked guilty and uncomfortable and miserably self-conscious. One chubby little boy was balanced on his grandma's lap, and while the wrinkled old lady talked fitfully with his parents, he stared with wideyed horror and fascination at the old people who watched him with envy and wonder.

My mother turned to us. "She's not here, obviously," she announced. "She's probably up in her room, as usual." We hurried down the corridor. A childlike wail cut through the air and I started. "What's that?" My father shrugged. "Some old man, probably, who's sick or lonely," he said. "You hear it once in awhile."

I shuddered. The smell of disinfectant was getting stronger. Several old people labored down the corridor, grasping the long wooden rail along the wall. One man in a red bathrobe was shuffling along and muttering to himself, but passing nurses and attendants acted as if he weren't there.

As we reached the main desk, a middle-aged nurse looked up sharply from her record book and amended her glance with a thin-lipped smile. "Hello there," she said to my mother. "Come to see you ma?" My mother nodded. "She's doing fine," the nurse added.

"Oh, I'm glad to hear it," Mom smiled back.

Dad pressed the elevator button.

"Does she know Gram?" I asked, surprised.

"Don't be silly," my mother muttered. The elevators doors opened. "She doesn't know my mother from Adam. If Gram were dying she'd still say she's 'doing fine.' She tells everybody the same thing." The elevator swooped gently up to the second floor. "It's Room 220, Deb. Don't be shocked."

Doors were open along the beige corridor and I couldn't resist glancing into the rooms. The first room was darkened, and I caught a glimpse of a frail old woman lying fully clothed on her bed, head tilted toward the ceiling. Lying motionless, she could have been dead. In the next room a nurse was scolding a weeping old man while an orderly mopped at a puddle in front of the bed. I turned my head quickly to the other side of the corridor. In Room 216, two middle-aged ladies chattered at a thin old man in a wheelchair. There were two old ladies in Room 218; one was lying in bed babbling quietly, the other stared at the pink and red tile on the floor.

At the door of Room 220, we hesitated. My mother arranged her face in a bright cheery smile, grasped the doorknob and breezed in. "Hello, Mom!" she sang. My father followed her but I hung back, suddenly apprehensive. I wanted to whisper that I'd wait for them in the car, but Dad turned to me and said, "C'mon, Debbie." Then Mom said gaily to Gram, "Mom, Debbie came to see you today. Look, here she is," and I had no choice but to enter the room.

It was small, pale green and dim, even with the yellow and green curtains pushed all the way to the sides of the window. Flanking two neatly made beds with dark green institutional covers were two formica topped night tables. My father was standing by the closet door, and Mom was seated on the bed nearest the window, next to a small dark figure.

"Hi, Gram," I said softly.

Gram turned to me slowly and my stomach contracted. Her face was thin and pinched and covered with wrinkles. Her eyes, always bright and alert, were dulled. She looked wasted, shrunken. Her hands lay motionless in her lap, as neatly as if someone had arranged them. She stared at me and I stood in the doorway, unable to move.

"That's Debbie, Mom, my big girl," my mother said. A bright, artificial smile seemed to paralyze the lower half of her face. "She's been away at school, you know. She's almost nineteen now. Hasn't she grown up?"

My father reached out and touched my stiff shoulder. "Go give Gram a kiss, Debbie," he prompted. I moved toward Gram and planted a kiss on her withered cheek. Around her hung an unfamiliar papery dry smell, and wisps of yellowed hair strayed from her bun. She kept staring at me. There was no recognition in her eyes.

"You know Debbie, Mom," my mother urged. She motioned for me to sit on the other side of Gram and leaned across her to tell me, "Well, at least she knows you're one of hers. Just talk nicely to her and smile and kiss her, and she'll be satisfied. We really can't expect anything more." I was shocked. How could she discuss Gram so casually when Gram was sitting right between us?

My father mistook my shocked silence for shyness. "Go on, Deb, talk to her," he directed. "Ask her how she is. Tell her about school, anything."

"Gram," I began. She turned to me politely.

An attendant wheeled a cart into the room. It was loaded with paper plates of cookies and dozens of tiny cups. "Juice or milk?" she droned.

"We'll have milk, I think. All right, Mom?" my mother asked. Gram nodded, and the attendant handed Gram a paper cup and a cookie and wheeled the cart out again. Gram held the cup in her trembling hands—they were as clawlike as those of the old lady downstairs—and sipped the milk. "Do they serve milk and cookies every day?" I asked.

My mother laughed shortly. "No dear," she said. "Only on Sundays, to impress the visitors." She patted Gram's hand and leaned over to open the drawer of Gram's night table. "Well, Mom," she said brightly, "and where did you put your dirty things this week? Let's see—ah yes, here's a bunch of them, right in with the clean ones. You know, dear," she said, extracting a few pairs of soiled pink cotton bloomers from the drawer and dropping them on the floor, "I wish you wouldn't mix the dirty things with the clean ones." An unmistakable odor came from the discarded clothes and I bit my lip. Gram used to be so meticulous that she would wash her hands even before she gardened.

"Well, that's the last of it, I think," Mom said, tossing a soiled lacy slip onto the pile. "And next week I'll bring them back to you, Mom, all nice and fresh." Gram was watching carefully as Mom gathered the dirty clothes into a plastic laundry bag. "Look how she's watching me, Debbie," my mother said. "They steal things left and right here. Look at her. She wants to make sure I'm not a crook." Gram gazed at my mother as if she hadn't heard what Mom had just said. I wanted to grab her and squeeze her tight until she protested, like she used to do, that I'd break her bones if I kept her in such a bear hug. But only her polite smile, I was sure, would answer me. I was a stranger to her, and my Gram was a stranger to me.

"Ralph," my mother was saying softly to my father. "Would you mind. . .?" He nodded and slipped out of the room, closing the door behind him. "I just want to change her," Mom explained to me. She bent and sniffed near Gram's armpits. I winced; Gram didn't. "Mmm," my mother said and began to unbutton Gram's navy blue dress. "I think you should change your clothes a little more often, Mom." I lowered my eyes, too embarrassed to watch. I started to move off the bed and Mom said, "Oh, Deb, that's all right. It's just that Gram doesn't like being undressed if there is a man in the room. That's all."

I ventured, "Don't the nurses take care of Gram's clothes and stuff?"

"Don't be silly," she grunted. She pulled a pink lace slip over Gram's head. As she bent to unhook Gram's corset she said. "These attendants don't do anything for anyone unless you tip them very well, which I for one—here, Mom, here's a fresh bra for you—refuse to do. Aside from seeing that most of the patients get a bath once a week or so, and they skip the ones that give them any trouble, they just pass the cookies and juice and mop the floor and look busy when the relatives come. Mom, pick up your arms, dear, and let me get this slip over your head. And if you want any kind of care at all, Deb," she continued, "you have to hire a private nurse. Get me one of those dark dresses from the right-hand side of the closet, will you? That's fine, thanks." She slipped the dress over Gram's head, stood up and beamed at Gram. "There now, you're all fresh and clean. Isn't that better?" Gram nodded mechanically and smiled at no one in particular. "See, Deb, she understands, but she doesn't respond."

Then give her the courtesy, I wanted to shout, of not talking right through her. You treat her like a baby, that's bad enough, but then you act as if she's not even here. Mom patted my hand, unaware of my bursting emotions and said, "Talk to her, Debbie. I want to find the head nurse." She stood up and put her hands lightly on Gram's shoulders. "Mom, Deb wants to tell you about school. It's very interesting and she has a lot to talk to you about. I won't be gone long." She walked out of the room, and Gram and I were left alone.

We faced each other. I smiled at Gram experimentally and her polite smile popped back at me. "I like college," I blurted.

Gram nodded. "What a big girl you are," she said in the tone she used when I was seven and eight.

I swallowed. "It's very far away, you know. It's about 400 miles away." She was still nodding. "I live in a dormitory with lots of other girls."

"Momma lets you go so far away from home."

I was stymied. "Well, I go to school there. Mom knows. It's all right."

"Oh." She was nodding again, uncomprehendingly. Her eyes were mild, passive.

"I have tons of work," I plunged on, "especially in chem—chemistry, I mean. And I'm taking French, too. Next term I'll be taking lit—I mean, a literature course." I stopped. She was still watching me, but her eyes were cloudy again. "What a big girl you are."

I started again, slowly. She kept her eyes on me. I talked on about my roommate and professors and the boys I was dating. She never stopped me. She just sat, her wrinkled hands clasped in her lap, nodding and smiling until my throat became so constricted I stammered to a halt.

"And I missed you, Gram," I said. I threw my arms around her and hugged her fiercely. Slowly her hands came up from her lap and her arms went around me.

I didn't hear my parents come in until my father cleared his throat. I turned then and saw them and the spare-looking head nurse with them. I dropped my arms almost guiltily and took one of Gram's dry hands in mine. My mother turned to the nurse and pointed to the laundry bag leaning against the closet.

"You see," she said to the starched nurse, "I just found all these dirty things in her night table and I just took this dress off her back a minute ago. I wish that someone would make sure that she's changed at least every three days. She's really a very clean woman," she said, looking directly into the woman's small brown eyes, "and I know she doesn't enjoy being filthy. Could you see to it, please?"

The nurse cast a sour glance at the laundry and nodded. "I'll take care of it, ma'am. It's a shame isn't it, that they get so dirty when they get old, after they have been clean all their lives?" She leaned toward Gram. "Now, Mrs. Reed, you be good," she admonished, and turning on her white shoes, walked out the door. Dad said to me, "Mom asks someone every week to see that Gram is kept clean, and nothing ever happens. And nothing will happen, Betty," he turned to my mother, "until you face the facts and start tipping."

My mother picked up the laundry bag. "Oh, Ralph," she said tiredly, "leave me alone. If we had to start tipping everybody for every little thing we'd be out of money in no time flat. And I'll bet you she'd still be wearing dirty underwear." My father didn't answer. I moved closer to Gram and put my other arm around her as if to protect her—from what, I wasn't sure.

My father looked at his watch. "It's getting late," he reminded my mother. "I know," she said. She leaned over Gram and kissed her on the forehead. "Mom, we have to leave now," she said. "I'll be here next week with your clean laundry and some more things and," she lowered her voice, "don't let them take anything away from you."

She glanced at me. "Go on, Deb," she said, "Kiss Gram goodbye."

I threw my arms around Gram again and felt her hug me in return. I rested my cheek against hers for a minute, aware that the fresh smell of the clean clothes contrasted with the faint papery smell of her skin, and for a minute the old love came swooping back to me. Then Mom tapped me on the shoulder and said, "Debbie," in a voice choked with the precarious presence of tears, and I got up. "Be good, Mom," my mother said. Dad came over to the bed and when he bent down to kiss her, she grabbed his coatsleeve and said quickly, "I'll walk you to the door."

Gram took small, unsure steps, as if she had forgotten how to walk and I remembered how she used to stride along the street with me beside her scrabbling vainly to keep up. Now she leaned as heavily on me as she did on my father. When we reached the elevator she was almost out of breath, but she managed to give us each a squeeze. "Thank you for coming," she said, as if we had been visiting her in her own house.

"We'll be back next week," my mother promised, and then she looked at me. I nodded. "And Debbie will come too," she added. "Oh look, the elevator is here already. Goodbye, Mom," she called. As the doors closed, Gram raised her hand and tentatively waved goodbye.

We hurried past the big recreation room. I peeped in again. The visitors had departed; the little blond cherub was gone, too. Only the old people and the attendants were left. Somebody had switched on the television, but nobody was watching. We stepped out into the cold.

With typical winter perfidy, the sun had disappeared behind a bank of mottled grey clouds and the air was knife sharp. I inhaled deeply, relieved that the stench of the Home was out of my nostrils, and ran ahead to the car. I had a peculiar sense of freedom, of being let out of a cage, and I felt painfully sorry for all the poor old people whom we had left behind.

In the car, my mother turned to me. The brittle smile was gone from her face and she looked exhausted. "Well, Deb, what did you think?" I looked out at the street. "It's awful," I said flatly. "It's horrible and ugly and smelly and I can't understand," my voice rose, "how you can let Gram be so miserable!" My mother turned her head slightly so I couldn't look directly into her eyes. My father glanced away from the icy street long enough to give Mom a look of compassion.

"We know, Deb," he said mildly. "We know. But there's really nothing else to do."

"Did you see all those other people?" I persisted. I was speaking to the back of my mother's head now. "They're sick and crippled and much worse off than Gram. Didn't she manage all the way to the elevator?" I hesitated. They were going to tell me that I didn't understand. But I couldn't bear to think of Gram wasting her life away in that overpriced prison, and I was horrified to think that my parents could shrug off so lightly the responsibility of caring for Gram. "I think we should take Gram to live with us."

A silence enveloped us. My mother sighed. "Darling," she said patiently, "I've explained to you why it's impossible. We can't give her the care she's getting at. . . ."

I interrupted her. "Oh come on, Mom! Don't tell me Gram's well off in that awful place."

"Debbie," my father said, "do you know what it would be like if we took Gram in? We'd all be nervous no matter how hard we'd try. We couldn't avoid the friction, Deb, can't you see?" He pulled into the driveway and the discussion was over.

My mother said something to me as we climbed the backstairs but I did not answer. I was too busy thinking about Gram's plight; it seemed incredibly selfish of the rest of the family to ignore it. I stumbled into my room, slammed the door, and flopped down on my bed. "It's so unfair," I said to myself. I thought of everything I had seen today. I couldn't let my Gram go through that. I would have to make my parents see that no sacrifice would be too great to have Gram in the house.

I lay back on the bed, planning. Oh, it would be hard at first, but we could manage. Mom was exaggerating. If she wanted to go shopping or something she could ask the neighbors to look in on Gram. They wouldn't mind.

And then, of course, I'd be able to keep Gram company during the summer. I'd be willing to stay home with her; we could even go to the beach together. Gram and Grampa used to take Jimmy and me. The more immediate problem was arranging living space for Gram.

I slipped off the bed and surveyed my room. It might be a little crowded, but we could squeeze another bed between my bed and the closet. There would be enough closet space for Gram if I pushed my clothes over, and I could empty one of my drawers for her. She wouldn't need more; she always said clothes weren't important to her, that what mattered was her family. I felt immeasurably guilty about the fact that I had paid so little attention to what had happened.

"Maybe I should put my bed next to the closet," I mused. When I came home late after a date I wouldn't want to wake Gram by climbing all over the room to put my things away. And, I realized, I would have to keep my room neater than it usually was. Disorder had always bothered Gram. My mind suddenly flashed back to the scene this afternoon of Mom foraging through Gram's night table to find her dirty laundry. It was so unbelievable; my Gram, who was always so meticulous.

What if she would do the same thing here? What if she couldn't remember which drawer was hers and hid her soiled things in one of my drawers? I shook my head to rid myself of the unpleasant thought. The only thing to do would be to mark off Gram's drawer so she would know which was hers and leave my things alone.

But she forgets easily now, I reminded myself. What could prevent her from forgetting which drawer belongs to her? Especially when she's tired and she wants to go to bed at night. . . .

Night. One of my favorite habits was to stay up far into the night, reading, listening to my little FM, writing poetry. And I liked to sleep late. I wouldn't be able to do any of that. Gram had always practiced early-to-bed-early-to-rise, and I'd be sure to disturb her if I wanted to stay up until three or four in the morning. Even if I didn't disturb her sleep I'd feel restricted by another person's presence, and what I loved about midnight and hours beyond was the serenity and freedom I felt then. Gram's puttering around in the early morning would wake me for sure, and I hated to be wakened before I wanted to get up. At least in the Home no one would disturb her sleep.

I slid the closet door shut. The Home was clean, they kept it very neat. Of course the smell was another matter, but then you could get used to almost anything. Hadn't I been able to adjust to the awful stink of the chem lab at school? Gram was all right at the Home. She had privacy, food, medical care if she needed it, and other old people near her if she wanted their company, which was more than we could offer her. It would be wrong to uproot her again and make her adjust to another new environment. Really, if the family would only visit her more, she would have everything.

I looked over my room once more and walked out, shutting the door behind me. "Mom," I would tell my mother when I got the kitchen, "you really should speak to Uncle Joe and Uncle Ed about visiting Gram more often. They ought to feel some responsibility toward her, too. It's not right, not right at all."

The Ashtray

Mr. Barker added his morning coffee cup to the small pile of last night's supper dishes in the sink, and wondered what to do next. He looked out the kitchen window of his small two-room apartment down into the grey alley below. He had a bird's eye view of untidy garbage pails, broken furniture, and an assortment of old bottles, cans, and newspapers. Despite the ugly scene, the jagged bits of sunshine splintering the greyness invited him outdoors.

Well, maybe he'd do a bit of shopping for his supper. Where was his wallet? He went back to the bedroom to search his jacket pocket. Not there! Instead, he felt a round, lumpy object and withdrawing it, beheld in his hands a freshly fired, beautifully glazed ashtray. Where had this come from? He couldn't recall buying it. Oh yes, this looked like something from the pottery class at the senior citizens center. Had he made it? It certainly was well done! He couldn't quite remember making this one, though. He could recall the feel of soft clay in his fingers . . . the power of shaping it . . . struggling with it until it looked like something you wanted. He enjoyed doing that! Ah—there had been a time, there had been a time . . . he had shaped many things, especially cloth. Making a pattern was no easy job, but he was an artist. He could take a piece of cloth, any kind of cloth, and he could cut it and twist it and pin it and shape it until it looked exactly as his mind's eye had seen it.

He'd never forget the day a new customer came into the dress shop where he worked. There was a hump on her back, and one shoulder was quite a bit higher than the other. Could he fit a dress for her? Could he? He had fashioned a dress for her that had really changed the way she looked. She needed it for her son's wedding, and when she tried it on, finished, she was radiant! "Thank you, thank you," she had said, "I was ashamed to go to my own son's wedding. But now, the way I look in this dress, I'll be proud to be seen!"

Mr. Barker glowed, remembering. He had felt so proud of himself that day. Proud to be able to do something like that . . . proud of his talent . . . his power to make things.

Oh yes, he was an artist all right. He had pictures in his mind all the time! But it was a long time since he had worked at it . . . years . . . and a long time since anyone had noticed what he could do. Well, he must have made this ashtray recently. He took the bright blue dish and went to place it in his kitchen cupboard. Reaching up, he was surprised to see five or six other brightly glazed pottery pieces sitting on the shelf. Where had they all come from? Thinking hard, he seemed to remember carrying them home from the crafts shop a few weeks ago. Well, he'd save them for the holidays. Give them to his children and grandchildren as gifts. They, at least, would be proud to have a piece of his work.

His work. He turned to look at three newly hung pictures on the wall. All his—painted last summer in the art class in the park. How beautiful the trees had been! He had stared and stared for so many hours at the twisted branches, heavy with delicate greenery—until he thought he would never forget the sight. He hardly remembered the task of the painting—just the pleasure of drinking in the beauty of the scene. Bending closer to look at the pictures, he frowned as he noticed signatures in the lower right-hand corner. Two of them read O'Brien, a third one read Seeman. By golly—what right did those men have to put their names on his pictures? They must have done it when the pictures were drying in the shop. Angrily he wondered how he could blot out the names without spoiling the paintings themselves. Better ask Mr. Lewis, the art teacher, next time he saw him.

Now—when would that be? What was today anyway? Monday? Friday? If it was Monday, then he would have seen his children yesterday—they always saw him on Sundays. Had he been with them yesterday? He couldn't recall. But if today was Friday, then he'd have been at the center yesterday . . . and he couldn't remember that either! He looked at the calendar hanging on the wall—but it was a monthly calendar. He could tell it was October, all right, but what week was it, and what day? Panic seized him. What if this were Tuesday or Thursday, the days he went to the center? He wouldn't want to miss his day there!

Looking for clues, his eyes went to the clock. So much time seemed to have passed since he had found the blue ashtray! But it was less than ten minutes. How slowly time could drag . . . oh, he sighed and slipped on the jacket.

Now, why was it he had pulled out that jacket? He couldn't quite remember why he was standing here, ready to leave the house. Automatically, he groped for his wallet but it wasn't in his pockets. Where could he have put it? He walked round and round the small apartment, opening and shutting drawers and closet doors . . . digging into the pockets of his old winter coat. . . .

He became more and more anxious. Where could that wallet be? How could he walk out of the house without it? His housekey was in the change purse.

Sweat glistened on his forehead as he searched and searched. Finally, in frustration, he sat down despondently—a small, white-haired man—frightened and defeated.

What should he do now? Beside the telephone, in large, easily read print, hung the phone number of the bookstore where his daughter worked. Almost desperately, he lifted the phone and dialed.

"Hello, book shop," Flossie's voice always sang a little when she answered the telephone. It lifted his spirits just to hear her.

He put a smile into his own voice. "Hello, my dear. It's your father."

"Papa, are you all right?"

He loved and hated the quick note of concern that crept into her voice when he called her at work. He realized that she worried about him. He also realized that any call from him might mean a problem for her.

"Nothing wrong, Flossie, nothing wrong," he said cheerily. "How are you? And the children?"

"Papa, I just spoke with you last night. Nothing has changed since last night!" a slight tone of impatience crept into her voice, now that she knew he was all right. "Why are you calling?"

How could he answer. Should he tell her he'd forgotten what day this was . . . that he couldn't find his wallet . . . that he was ready to go out but couldn't remember why . . . that he'd found a strange ashtray in his pocket and didn't know how it got there . . . what was he to answer?

Craftily, he said. "Well, my dear, I'm just going out for a little while. I thought maybe, if you called me, and didn't find me home, you would worry."

"Oh, thank you, Papa. That's nice of you. Where are you going?" then added quickly, "Of course, today is Thursday, and you're getting ready to go to the center."

Ahah—thought Mr. Barker gleefully, then it was Thursday. I must have known it all along. Aloud, "Yes. That's right, I'll do a little shopping on the way, and I'll have my lunch at the center."

"Don't forget to take some money along." Flossie said, then added, "Not too much Papa. It's no good to carry too much extra with you. Anyone could lose money, you know."

"You're right, you're right. Let me see," he said into the telephone, "how much shall I take?"

"Take a few dollars," she suggested, "and leave the rest home. She lowered her voice almost to a whisper. "You remember, Papa, last Sunday we decided to put all your money away in a special place, so when you leave the house you wouldn't worry? Remember?"

Yes, by golly, he did remember. But where was that special place? He racked his brain. . . .

"Sure, sure," he said heartily into the telephone, "think I'd forget such a thing?"

"Papa," she said softly, "be sure you close the door of the linen closet before you leave the house. That way, it will be okay."

Of course, the linen closet! They had slipped a small bag of change and singles under the pile of sheets in the linen closet—so he would have carfare and shopping money for the whole week. That's where the wallet was!

He chided Flossie. 'What's the matter with you? Don't worry about me. I can take care of everything myself. I have to go now."

"Have a good day, Papa, I'll call you tonight."

"Goodbye, Flossie," he said gratefully.

"Goodbye." She hung up, satisfied that she had played the game again today . . . and Papa had won his round. Straightening her shoulders as if a huge load had rolled off her back, she turned to the waiting customer. . . .

Mr. Barker smiled as he hung up. Now he was set for the day. He slipped his wallet out from its hiding place, checked keys and money. Turning toward the mirror in the hall, he caught the first sight of himself that morning. He had not shaved. He was still wearing his pajama tops under the jacket; and he had been about to walk out wearing his slippers!

Barker, get hold of yourself! He shook his finger at the mirror. Briskly he went into the bathroom, shaved, cleaned his razor, wiped the sink carefully, put on a fresh shirt, found a better jacket, slipped on his street shoes. Then he took a paper shopping bag and, locking the door carefully behind him, left the building and stepped out into the street toward the bus stop.

He watched the streets carefully, as the bus carried him along. There was a time you could tell one street from another easily . . . the gay barbershop poles, the signs on the small stores, . . . you never missed your stop. Now, one street looked like another . . . the tall brick projects all the same —you had to watch carefully for the small black sign that read "Senior Citizens Center." One day he had missed it and had ridden all the way to the end of the line—feeling like a fool. The bus driver had looked at him as if he were an addled old man—and had insisted on collecting a second fare for the trip back.

He couldn't afford a double carfare, so it was necessary for Mr. Barker to watch very, very carefully as the bus wound its way to the senior center.

Entering the craft shop, he saw the slim figure of Mr. Lewis half-hidden inside the closet. Mr. Lewis was a gentle, soft-spoken young fellow who made you feel good just being with him. Even though he wore a beard, he never made you feel clumsy or foolish.

"Hello," Mr. Barker said jovially, "What are you doing in that closet?"

Mr. Lewis straightened up. "Hi," he said. "I'm looking for some lost pottery. Last week we fired a beautiful bright blue ashtray that Mrs. Johnson made, and it just seems to have disappeared."

Mr. Barker became uneasy as Mr. Lewis went on. "I seem to be getting awfully careless with things, lately," he said. "I'm missing some good work from the summer program, too. Some pictures. Some pottery. I don't know what I'll do when the people come to ask for them. I'm terribly ashamed. You folks put so much into the work you do—it's wrong for me to misplace it."

Mr. Barker listened with growing anxiety. Why did he feel so trapped, he wondered, and why were his palms suddenly sweating? He set down his shopping bag in the corner of the shop saying, "Don't worry, Mr. Lewis. You'll find them all. Everybody knows you do your best. No one will blame you."

But, for some reason, he began to feel terribly uncomfortable. Leaving his shopping bag behind, he sauntered out toward the lounge where he heard music and laughter. There was a nagging, nameless, uncomfortable feeling in his entire being all day. He spent the rest of the day away from the shop.

By five o'clock, people began to drift out of the building. Mr. Barker suddenly realized that he didn't have his shopping bag, and went to the receptionist.

"Mrs. Gold," he said, "please give me my shopping bag. I left it here when I came in."

"I'm sorry, Mr. Barker," she answered, "I don't have your shopping bag here."

"Please look," he insisted, "I brought it into the office when I came into the center."

"You didn't give it to me. Was there someone else here when you came in?"

"I don't know," he answered with growing impatience. "But I'm sure it's here, Mrs. Gold."

"Maybe you didn't bring it today," she offered.

"Yes, I did," he said—very angry now, sure he had brought the bag with him.

"Come into the office and look around," she invited.

He entered her office, searching through drawers and closet, muttering angrily. When he found nothing, he shouted, "Somebody took it. Who took it? Who took my shopping bag?"

In vain did the office staff, and the few people in the hall seek to calm him. Mr. Barker shouted loudly that his bag had been stolen . . . the office was responsible . . . what was the matter with them anyway, treating people this way!

Hearing the commotion, Mr. Lewis came to the hall. When he understood the problem, he came into the office, carrying the bag.

"Is this what you're looking for, Mr. Barker?"

Mr. Barker grabbed the bag. "You see," he shouted at Mrs. Gold, "I told you somebody took it. He took it . . . and you tried to make me think I didn't have it today. You can drive a man crazy that way!"

Mr. Lewis tried to set him straight. "You left it in the shop, yourself, Mr. Barker," he reminded the man gently. "Remember, you came in when I was looking for the lost pottery?"

"Well," Mr. Barker shouted, "I didn't take your pottery but you took my shopping bag."

Despite all efforts to soothe him, Mr. Barker left the building angry and disturbed, and took the bus home.

He unlocked his door and entered his apartment. With great care, he removed his wallet from his pocket and placed it inside the copper vase in the hallway. A good hiding place until tomorrow!

He fixed himself some supper, washed and dried the accumulated dishes in the sink. As he opened the kitchen closet to put the dishes away, he saw again the multicolored gleam of the pottery on the shelf.

Why did they distress him so, he wondered. He reached up for the blue ashtray. It was smooth and cool in his sweaty, trembling palm. He looked at it thoughtfully. Yes, he might have made it. He might have made all those lovely things. He knew how to make things. He was an artist . . . how dare anyone think . . . well, let them think. . . .

They were his. All of them. His.

Shura Saul

The Angry Giant

I knew a man once, tall and gaunt
Who hung his head against his hand
Whose mind was sure and strong and sage
But lived within a twisted cage
Of rage.

With brothers in a secret band
When he was young he fought the Czar
For freedom, justice, bread and beauty
Lived his life in noble duty
Knightly quest for right and truth . . .
Quixotic youth.

Then to the tundra banished
For an endless time.
To my listening ears it seemed
He told a tale a child dreamed
Of legendary years all vanished
Into history and rhyme.

He told me of the deeds they'd dared
Against their king. Of dangers shared
Of comrades' love—and one betrayed.
And how, suspicious and afraid
Dependent for their cause, their lives
Upon each other and their wives
They judged one of their own
To kill.

Half a century ago . . .
He is tormented still.

He told me of the maid he loved
How awkwardly he wooed and lost.
For warmth and woman how he'd thirst
But then his sacred cause came first
Its sacrifice and cost.

He mocked himself, demeaned himself
He mourned in muted mode.
The lifetime struggles of his soul
He measured meagerly
Within his rigid code.

Severe without repentance
Harsh in his self-hate
He tried and judged and damned himself
His blindness was his sentence
His blindness was his fate.

In troubled tones the tales he told
Would like some book of myths unfold
While underneath the weighted words
A frantic, furious river ran . . .
For now the knight is blind and old
A lonely giant
An angry man.

Shura Saul

The Marriage

"When I came to live in this home," Mr. Seeman said thoughtfully, "I thought my whole life was over. I didn't blame my children. They aren't so young anymore themselves—and they have their own troubles. Eddie had a heart attack. Rosie's husband is more out of work than working. I couldn't stand it to live alone anymore—and I couldn't live with them. So I figured— like an old horse, I'll put myself out to pasture and I came here."

Mrs. Belkin squeezed his hand affectionately. The two old people were sitting in the grape arbor on the grounds of the Home; enjoying the fragrance of the ripening grapes, basking in the gentle warmth of the late summer sun, listening to the faint buzzing of the bees as they clustered and rustled in the leaves. A small symphony of sounds surrounded them.

"I know," Mrs. Belkin said. She sang her words a little, drawing out the vowel like a descant to the muted chorus. "I know. It was the same with me. At first, I didn't mind it so much—living alone. The children came to visit, helped me a little with the shopping. But then, my vision got worse and worse . . . the children started to come running all the time . . . always worrying about me. Who wants to be a burden on the children? So I came here?"

Mr. Seeman said, somewhat proudly, "I did my own shopping until the last day. Even the cooking, the housework, All right, maybe a man isn't such a good housekeeper, but I managed. The worst was the loneliness. In the morning I used to push myself out of the bed. In the evening, ah, it was bad. Alone. Alone. I was so lonesome, Bella."

"Yes," she said. "Sometimes I used to wonder, why bother to wake up in the morning. Some weeks, except for a telephone call from the children, I didn't open my mouth to talk to another person."

"Well," he said, "it's not bad here. Clean. Respectable. But I'm not the same person, Bella. I lost something. I don't feel like a man anymore." He shook his head. "I'm not—like the children say—I'm not my own man."

"Don't say that, Sam. You are very much a man. A fine man."

"How lucky I am that I found you here," he answered.

"We are both lucky," she said.

"Bella, I love you."

She put her head on his shoulder and he reached for her hand. Bella said quietly, almost blurring her words, "Ah, Sam, if we had only met, somehow, before we came here. It might have been different for us.

"Would you have had me, Bella?"

"What do you mean?" she asked.

"I mean," he replied with some excitement, "Would you have married me?"

She didn't answer immediately. Then she said, "What are we, two children? Sam—we are two old people."

"Yes, but we are a man and a woman. We're old, but we're alive. I want you very much, Bella. I ask you— if you had met me before you came here, would you have accepted me as a husband?"

"Maybe," she said cautiously, "maybe. . . ."

He went on, his voice quickening. "We could have managed—you and I together. We could pool our small incomes . . . live in a small apartment . . . maybe have a woman to come in once in awhile and do the heavy cleaning. And we'd have each other . . . no more loneliness. Even our children would have been better off. Sometimes mine would come—sometimes yours. Grandchildren could have visited us. We could be living like people!"

She said dreamily, "That sounds lovely, Sam. So good."

Sam said with sudden passion, "Bella, why can't we do it now? We aren't dead yet!"

She lifted her head. "Do you think it's possible? How?"

Now he hesitated. "I'm not sure. What would the children say?"

"Let's ask them."

"I'm afraid."

They had both retreated. But the idea had been born and remained alive. It tugged at their consciousness, not to be denied. After a long silence, Sam said, "You know what, Bella. Let's think it over."

"Yes," she agreed, glowing and blushing a little. "We could think it over."

The sun was beginning to set. The grape arbor grew cool.

"Come," he said, "it's time to go inside."

* * *

Standing at the window of her colorful, softly cozy office, Mrs. Anton, the administrator of the Home, watched Mr. Seeman and Mrs. Belkin walking hand in hand toward the house. Mrs. Anton was a small, vibrant woman in her early sixties who raced around the immaculate Home in her space shoes, mothering the institution; smiling, frowning, praising, correcting, scolding, fixing, helping, . . . she was aware of every physical and psychological nook and cranny of "her Home." It was she who had introduced these two to each other when Mr. Seeman was first admitted. It was she who had known that the strong, gentle, bright woman would be just the right friend for this restless, uncertain newcomer. Now—as she watched them walking together toward her office, she could almost guess their concern. Her own heart jumped a little—in expectation.

The next moment she winced angrily as she noticed two white-uniformed staff members whispering behind cupped fingers, giggling and pointing at the old couple holding hands. Why did some people think life was over for the residents here? Why did they behave as if life, love, and sexual desire died within the elderly person who stepped inside the institution doorway? Why didn't they respect the hunger for life that. . . .

The knock on her door interrupted her mounting anger. She listened with interest as they talked with her haltingly . . . wonderingly describing their feelings for each other . . . then, with some hesitation, sharing their desire and despair.

"Why can't you get married?" Mrs. Anton urged.

"At our age?" Mr. Seeman asked, huskily.

"Here?" It was Bella, almost with anger.

"Certainly," Mrs. Anton said vigoriously. "At your age. Here. We certainly could give you your own room!"

After much beating round the bush, and groping for tactful words (lest Mrs. Anton feel rejected by them), they finally clarified for her that this wasn't what they wanted. They wanted a real life, a complete life, together. Oh, if only they had met before. . . .

Mrs. Anton helped them put some thoughts in order. Of course, whatever they did, they would want to talk it over with their children. She was sure their children would understand and cooperate. Mostly, she encouraged them to dream . . . to plan . . . to work out something that would seem right for them.

* * *

The morning of the wedding dawned bright and clear. Awakening, realizing that this was the day, Sam panicked.

"I'm sick," he told his roommate, Mr. Greenwald.

Greenwald laughed at him. "Bridegroom sickness," he diagnosed in his caustic, throaty voice.

"Greenwald, I'm telling you I'm sick. I can't go through with it."

Usually sarcastic and angry, Greenwald was surprisingly supportive. "Sam," he said, "you're only proving what a man you are. Seventeen or seventy, a man is afraid to get married. Can't you remember the first time, Sam?"

Sam grinned. "I remember," he said. "It was a nightmare. I wasn't sure if I was going to the chuppah or the sacrificial altar!"

Greenwald clapped him on the shoulder. "You see, you have the same sickness now. No man wants to give up his independence. But don't worry," he added, suddenly serious, "Bella Belkin is a good woman. She won't put a ring in your nose."

Sam rubbed his nose sheepishly. "Maybe, Greenwald, you could help me put on the jacket? It's getting late."

* * *

In the women's wing, Bella's roommates were acting like bridesmaids. She had made her own small hat and veil; Mrs. Zimmerman insisted on giving her a pair of matching gloves; Mrs. Rosen brought a small lapel pin for her blue velvet jacket; and the nurse on duty gave her a white linen handkerchief with blue tatting.

The wedding was in the synagogue of the Home. Children and grandchildren, staff and residents, gathered to hear the vows exchanged . . . to shed a silent tear as the cantor sang the ancient hymns to love. And in each listening heart there was a thrust of anxiety as the rabbi spoke briefly and beautifully of hope.

Bella and Sam moved through the ceremony as if they were dreaming it. Finally, the wedding was over. The wedding guests had danced, and everyone had sung the old Yiddish songs with their mixture of tears and gaiety. Sam's son, Eddie, drove them to the small new apartment which the children had found and furnished for them. Then Eddie kissed them both, and went home.

At last the newlyweds were alone—together. And it was real.

* * *

For three years, Sam and Bella lived like everyone else. They shopped and cooked, laughed and cried, were restless and content, took care of each other—and lived, together. Sam shopped and grumbled at the high prices . . . and found all sorts of things to worry and complain about. Bella scolded him and calmed him. They quarreled, made up, and loved. Together.

In good weather, they walked to the sunny park across the street, visiting with other elderly people in the neighborhood. In bad weather they sat before their television, hoping someone would come in to visit . . . being lonely . . . together.

Three golden years. Pleasant and unpleasant. Then Sam's vision began to fail, and Bella became increasingly frail. They decided to call Mrs. Anton.

They were ready now for her original offer. If she still had room for them, they would like to come back to the Home as a couple to live out the rest of their lives together.

And so they did.

Shura Saul

Neighbors: Vignette in Black and White

Katie McGrath's morning mail included a large manila envelope with an unfamiliar return address. Opening it, she withdrew a slim magazine and, as she unfolded it a small note fluttered to the floor. Stooping to pick it up, she noticed the picture on the cover and gasped "What in heaven's name. . . ." She opened the note quickly. It was typewritten and read simply: "Mr. Morris, whose picture is on the cover of our current issue, has requested this copy to be mailed to you. It is sent with the compliments of the Hospital Workers Union of New York."

Katie looked at the picture, reread the note, poured herself a second cup of coffee, smiled, and began to remember.

She and her husband Joe, both in their early seventies, lived in their own small house in a crowded neighborhood in the Bronx. Mr. Morris and his wife Ruth, tenants in the small house next door, were a quiet black couple in their middle sixties. Both couples were childless.

Katie's husband, Joe, still worked as a toolmaker in a small metal shop. Mr. Morris was a porter in a hospital. Although they lived next door to each other, the men rarely saw one another as their work schedules differed. However, Katie McGrath and Ruth Morris, the women, knew each other quite well. After several meetings in the supermarket, they began to shop together. They borrowed cups of sugar and flour, and soon began to share a second cup of coffee when they rested, in the morning, from household chores which were becoming increasingly difficult for them.

When Ruth began to complain of pains in her abdomen, it was the most natural thing for Katie to accompany her to the doctor, and to continue to do so as the trips became more frequent. Katie was an old hand at helping people, and knew many important things such as how to fill out hospitalization forms and where to get senior citizen information. Whenever Katie filled out a form for her, Ruth would say, "Thank you, my social worker!" and the two old women would laugh together.

As Ruth became more and more ill, Katie began to oversee more and more of her needs. Finally, when Ruth was hospitalized, it was Katie who visited her daily and found ways to make her comfortable. She would bring her reports to Mr. Morris and try to comfort him.

Mr. Morris would sit alone in his small apartment. Katie would bring him a cup of soup in the evening, a dish of stew, a piece of pie. Mr. Morris washed his own dishes, tidied up, imposed on no one. Joe tried once or twice to visit with him, but Mr. Morris was not very eager to talk. He knew his wife was very, very ill and that he could do little for her.

After Ruth died, and the formalities of death had been attended to— mostly by competent Katie—Mr. Morris secluded himself. He mourned deeply and in private. The McGrath's never interfered, but Katie kept a private watch over him.

Christmas Day, Joe and Katie donned their holiday best, selected a bottle of good wine, and rang the Morris doorbell. Mr. Morris dispelled their apprehensions by returning their "Merry Christmas" and inviting them in.

The apartment, though tidy, was bare and forlorn. Although months had passed since she died, Ruth's absence was sharply apparent. Mr. Morris, warmed by their friendliness and the wine, began to talk. First they talked of Ruth and how much he missed her.

"You're too alone," said Katie. "You need some company, friends."

"Well," he replied," it isn't too bad at work. I know lots of people in the hospital. Also, I can eat two meals there now, so that helps my food problem. Sometimes, after work, I have a beer with a few of the men but," he added quickly, "I'm not much for that you know. It's just hard to come home to an empty house."

There was a silence. For Katie and Joe, married over 50 years, this was the greatest fear. For one to lose the other. To remain alone.

Katie said, "I know, Mr. Morris."

After another silence, Mr. Morris then said, "But I have some more troubles now. Two of them at once. First of all, they're telling me at the hospital that I must retire."

Joe stiffened at these words. Next to losing Katie, this was what he dreaded the most. No matter how difficult he was finding his job now—getting up at 6 in the morning, traveling the subway to work and back five days a week . . . no matter how tired he was each evening, retiring earlier and earlier to feel ready for the next day's work! He felt lucky that in his trade, skilled toolmaking, experienced workers were few and he was still, at his age, able to hold down a full-time job!

Katie was soothing Mr. Morris. "Listen," she said, "Maybe that's not so bad. Maybe it's time you took it a little easier."

"Well, maybe," Mr. Morris said glumly, "but my next problem is even worse. The landlord is selling this house, and the new owners want my apartment. Where will I go? Where can I move—especially with rents so high now, and me retiring!"

Joe was too upset to respond. How could a man cope with so many blows at once! But Katie said, "Let me think about that, Mr. Morris. Every problem must have some solution. Let's sleep on it, and see what we come up with for you!"

Her words cheered both men, and her husband reached over for the wine bottle, refilled the three glasses, and said, "Meantime, Mr. Morris—a happy, healthy Christmas! And let's see a little more of you from now on!" And they drank to that.

Mr. Morris was not one to visit much, but he did come for New Year dinner, dressed in his best, with a bottle of rye for his hosts. After the dishes were cleared Katie said, "Mr. Morris, I've been doing some thinking and I have an idea. Are you a member of a union?"

"Oh yes," he replied. "I'm not too worried about money. The union will give me a small pension and then, of course, there's social security."

"But I think the union might be able to help you with more than that," Katie told him. "Don't they have a social service department, or a retirement counseling program. I've read that some unions do. Does yours?"

Mr. Morris's eyes lit up. "I think you are right," he said. "I don't pay much attention to these things but I did see something in the shop bulletin. I'm going to ask my shop steward."

With Katie's encouragement, he followed through and found that his union did, indeed, have such a service which included a housing plan for their retired members.

It hadn't been difficult to help him move. His furnishings were sparse, his belongings few. Before he left, the neighbors shared a meal and wished each other well. Mr. Morris gave Katie a small bible that had been Ruth's. Katie accepted it with tears and whispered that she would treasure it.

Mr. Morris moved away quietly. He telephoned Katie once to tell her the apartment was sunny, warm, and clean. There were a few other retired workers from his union in the building, and he found them friendly. Soft-spoken Mr. Morris had found a new, comfortable home for himself.

Katie looked at the magazine cover and reread the caption: "Retired member of hospital workers union now living in low income housing under new union program." Mr. Morris was smiling, sitting in a simple, but comfortable looking one-room apartment.

"Hello, old neighbor," she whispered with a small, tearful grin, "You haven't done too badly, have you?"

Shura Saul

Old People Talk About Sex

Sidney R. Saul

This is a psychotherapist's record of a discussion by a psychotherapy group in a nursing home. The group consists of 10 elderly men and women who meet weekly to discuss their concerns and to help each other, with the aid of the therapist, in coping with their living problems at the institution. Several of these people were disoriented when they first joined the group . . . even to the point of confusing time and place. All of them were depressed, angry, withdrawn and/or asocial in their behavior. For each of them, the admitting diagnosis included terms such as "organic mental syndrome," "senile psychosis," "senility." However, each of these people showed a functional level of communication that suggested their referral to the group. The thrust of treatment is toward supporting and restoring mental health, to help each person find himself and his essential humanity within his difficult life circumstances.

At this session, 6 of the 10 group members participated actively in the portion of the discussion reproduced below. These 6 people were:

Mr. Curtis. A dignified black gentlemen, age 75, ambulatory and competent in physical self-care and all activities of daily living. Mr. Curtis had been referred to the nursing home from the geriatric unit of a state mental hospital. On admission, he was withdrawn and very depressed. Admitting diagnosis included "organic mental syndrome."

Mr. Reilly. A severely handicapped, poststroke gentleman, age 80; visually handicapped and in need of assistance in every aspect of physical care, including feeding. He had been admitted from home, extremely disoriented and very angry. Admitting diagnosis included "senility."

Miss Healy. Partially ambulatory, pleasant-faced, black woman, age 82. She sits in a wheelchair and needs assistance in many activities of daily living. Her admitting diagnosis, in addition to her physical problems, included "senile psychosis."

Mrs. Waters.   An angry, hostile, black woman, age 78, referred to nursing home from state mental hospital. She is ambulatory (with walker) and semicompetent in physical self care. Her admitting diagnosis included "senile psychosis."

Mr. Thomas.   Ambulatory man in his late sixties. He has physical problems requiring nursing care, but he is competent in activities of daily living. He had been referred to the group because he had been very depressed, uncommunicative, and showed a great deal of memory loss. Admitting diagnosis included "organic mental syndrome."

Mr. Peters.   Alert, ambulatory gentleman, age 84. He was referred to the group because he was depressed, anxious and very guilty about his blind, dying wife who was also a patient in the same home. Mr. Peters gave his wife a great deal of help and attention, and needed the supportive treatment of this group program. His admitting diagnosis included "senility."

* * *

The group, and Miss Helen (assisting staff member), was already assembled when I entered the room. I had been detained by several emergencies elsewhere in the house, and I was late. Mr. Reilly greeted me first.

Mr. Reilly.   Good morning, Doctor. It's Friday and it is ten past ten. You are ten minutes late.

(There is general agreement and humorous chafing. I am delighted. This from a group which, 10 sessions ago, had hardly been able to recall day, date, or time! I explain that I've been called to attend to several emergencies, and I apologize for my lateness.)

Miss Helen.   Well, you aren't the only one to be late today, Doctor. Miss Healy was a little late, too, as she insisted on putting on a pretty dress for you. I couldn't convince her that it wasn't necessary. She insisted!

Therapist.   Miss Healy, you do look lovely this morning. But a woman as beautiful as you doesn't need fancy clothes. You just shine!

Miss Healy.   (Smiling with pleasure at the compliment) You should see how cute Mrs. Landon looked, up on my floor this morning. She and Mr. Rosen were holding hands, walking up and down the hall.

Mr. Peters.   They are always looking for a place to smooch! (He laughs.)

Mr. Curtis.   (Also laughing, but very uncomfortable) Those two are both "senile" and they don't know what they're doing.

(The whole group laughs nervously. Some begin to blush. The subject of sex is now opened, for the first time, in this group, and I am quick to take advantage of it as a subject for further discussion.)

Therapist.   There is something you can explain to me about this subject that most people like to "sweep under the rug." I'd like to know what you do about sex? How do you handle your sexual desires, living here in the nursing home?

(There is more nervous giggling and looks of astonishment appear on their faces.)

Miss Healy.   Us? Our sexual desires???

Mr. Curtis.   Yes, us. Just because we are old doesn't mean we have no desires!

(Mr. Reilly begins to fidget and I ask him if this discussion is bothering him.)

Mr. Reilly.   Yes. Sex is a private subject and it bothers me to talk about it in public. It is nobody's business.

Therapist.   Mr. Reilly, I don't mean for you to discuss your personal sex practices. You are right. That is private. We are talking about the general situation for people living in an institution.

Mr. Reilly.   Well, I suppose that is something we can talk about (pauses a moment). People in an institution need privacy.

(Mr. Thomas, an ex-seaman, has been listening very intently but has not said a word. I know he had been involved in incidents in which he and a consenting female had engaged in sexual activity and had been embarrassed by the staff.)

Therapist.   Mr. Thomas, what is your opinion?

Mr. Thomas.   I think that if two grown-ups feel they would like to enjoy sex, it is their business, and the staff should understand and not get so upset about it!

(Mrs. Waters, who is usually very passive, lackadaisical, and sleepy in the group, had become quite alert. Her eyes open wide. She leans forward, and through her body motions begins to participate in the discussion.)

Therapist.   And what is your opinion, Mrs. Waters?

Mrs. Waters.   Meeeeee? Why me? (Her drawling tone is excited and loud.)

Mr. Curtis.   (Rather belligerent—a rare expression of his covert anger) Yes you! Because you are no different from anybody else. You also have feelings and thoughts and we want to hear them. What's your opinion?

(Mrs. Waters, characteristically, cocks her head, glares angrily at Mr. Curtis, but refuses to reply.)

Miss Healy.   (Indignantly) Well, I'll tell you. I'd never get myself involved that way!

Therapist.   Never? Have you *ever* had a suitor, Miss Healy?

Miss Healy.   A suitor, yes. But never a lover.

Therapist. Are you telling us that in your more-than-80 years of life you never had a sexual experience?

Miss Healy. That's right.

Mr. Reilly. (Turns slowly toward her until he is looking straight into her eyes)
I don't believe a word you are saying!

Miss Healy. It's true. I wouldn't lie! Besides, what difference would it make at my age, now. Why don't you believe me?

Mr. Reilly. Because sex is beautiful and it is human. You are too beautiful and human a person not to have had the experience. Therefore, I don't believe a word you are saying.

(Miss Healy leans back. She is thoughtful and rather quiet. We continue.)

Therapist. Mr. Reilly, I agree with you, sex is beautiful and it is human. What about the human, sexual needs of people who live in an institution?

Mr. Curtis. I suppose, if people know what they are doing—you know—if they are in their rights minds (Points to his head) not all mixed up, it is all right.

Mr. Peters. Yes, but what about people like Mr. Josephs and Mrs. Rubens? (Both not members of this group) He's always taking his "thing" out and giving it to the ladies. Poor Miss Rubens doesn't know what's going on so she takes it in her hand. (He begins to laugh) The other day she took it and pulled him halfway across the room. He yelled so loud you would think he was being murdered. What about that kind of situation?

(The laughter is general. It eases the group's tension over this kind of discussion of a "taboo" subject. The question is repeated: What about sexual contact among people in an institution?)

Mr. Thomas. The staff gets so upset, they don't even let you hold hands.

Therapist. What should the staff do?

Mr. Curtis. Well, if both people are in their right minds, and both are willing, the staff should leave them alone.

Therapist. And what about someone like Mrs. Rubens, who is quite disoriented and doesn't know what is happening sometimes?

Miss Healy. (With great dignity) Such a woman needs to be protected.

Mr. Curtis. (With equal dignity) Some of the men need protection too.

Therapist. Then, what are we saying about this matter?

Mr. Reilly. (Looks around at the group and speaks clearly and precisely)
We are saying that it is human to have sexual feelings. If two people are able to decide they want to enjoy it, they should be given their privacy, but some people need to be protected.

(The group members and their agreement with this summation of their discussion. Some of the group members seem surprised at Mr. Reilly's leadership and initiative . . . he has not been this active in the discussions heretofore.)

Therapist. (Noting their surprised reaction at Mr. Reilly's excellent summary) Why is everyone so startled? What do you think happened here today?

(There is a brief silence. It is clear that everyone is thinking actively, trying to respond to the question. Miss Healy replies first.)

Miss Healy.   Dr. Saul, I think we awakened Mr. Reilly's intellect!

(The group relaxes at this reply. They nod and smile in agreement. Mr. Reilly beams and looks very pleased with himself. So does the rest of the group. *Now*, Mr. Jones, whose body motions have shown intense interest in the discussion, but who has not contributed verbally, suddenly looks at his watch. Mr. Jones is a man who is usually quite disoriented as to time, date, and place. He looks at his watch and announces to the group. . . .)

Mr. Jones.   I think it is time to go to lunch.

Therapist.   Thanks for reminding us, Mr. Jones. We almost forgot.
    (We all help each other out of the room.)

Change, Hope and Struggle

The Haze Begins to Clear

*(Based on thoughts expressed in discussion with
residents at a home for aged blind people.)*

When I lost my vision
When I became blind
The shock of it exploded in my mind
And left a smokey haze behind
Beclouding intellect and thought

And now, here we sit
Talking together a little bit
Sharing the woe that this explosion wrought

Here, within this group, I find
I'm freed somewhat from fear
The talk is warm
The new found friendship dear

And softly, gently now
The haze begins to clear . . .

Shura Saul

Be Friendly

When Mary Brenner reported for her first day of work in the apartment house, she knew immediately that the dishevelled white-haired lady in the lobby was Mrs. Redmont. She had been told about the slender old woman who always sat there, glum and lonely. But she had not been prepared for the dirty black dress with the untidy slip hanging beneath the torn hem. She had not been adequately warned about the curved despondent shoulders, the small head hanging sadly to one side, the wrinkled, haggard face. And she was particularly shocked at the stark blue eyes that stared hungrily into the emptiness around her.

Mary nodded a pleasant good morning and entered the office, where she hung up her coat and started the coffee. The sunny room was filled with plants and bright pictures. Mrs. Bergson, the housing manager, was to be gone for six months and she, the new secretary, had been briefed to fill in for her.

"Be friendly," Mrs. Bergson had told her, "it's part of your job to let the tenants feel they can count on you for certain little things. We provide special housing for the elderly, and we encourage independence . . . but everyone needs a little help sometimes. I'm so glad you're taking this job, I can see you'll be nice to them."

Mary dusted the immaculate desk, watered the plants, and wondered about Mrs. Redmont. She'd been told that this old lady had come home from a hospital about two months ago (what kind of hospital? Mary wondered), and she seemed very, very lost. At first, some of the tenants had tried to be friendly, but she never let them come into her apartment where she lived alone. She pushed off their advances, and so they got tired of trying to be nice. Now, they were distressed and angry about her. Mary could see that her appearance would be frightening and disturbing to others. It certainly disturbed her.

As soon as she began typing, the telephone rang. It was Mrs. Gerson, apartment 5B, demanding—in clipped tones—to know whether this was the new secretary. Mary said yes, and what could she do for her.

"I just want to tell you that Mrs. Redmont is sitting in the lobby again. I don't know if anyone told you, but really, she should be sent upstairs. She makes this place look like an institution. It's terrible, Miss . . . what is your name anyway?"

"My name is Mary Brenner."

"Well, Miss . . . is it Miss or Mrs?"

"Mrs. Brenner, but you can call me Mary."

"Well, Mary—we really don't want the whole neighborhood to think, just because elderly people live in this apartment house, that we're all mental patients. Send her upstairs, right away."

Mary flinched at the commanding, angry voice—the disdainful words. "Don't worry, Mrs. Gerson," she said. "I'll take care of it."

She put the receiver down softly and went out to introduce herself to the lonely, rigid old woman. Mrs. Redmond answered politely, but stiffly, drawing away from the outstretched hand. She refused the offer of a cup of coffee. Troubled, Mary returned to her typing. A few minutes later, she noticed that Mrs. Redmont had left the lobby.

Each day it was the same. As soon as Mary began her typing, one of the upstairs tenants would call, angrily demanding that Mrs. Redmont be sent upstairs. Mrs. Redmont always left, quietly, shortly after the phone call, even though Mary never told her anything about them. Mary began to realize that Mrs. Redmont was quite aware of the nature and content of the calls . . . of the feelings of the tenants.

It would appear then—Mary mused when she had connected Mrs. Redmont's exit from the lobby with the telephone calls—that this lady is not quite as detached as she seems to be. In fact, she continued to herself, she's quite aware . . . and sensitive about things.

One morning, hearing agitated voices at the mailbox, Mary went to investigate. The postman was grumbling to Mrs. Gerson.

"Look at this mailbox. It's so jammed up with old mail, I can't put anything else into it. Why the devil doesn't she take out her mail?"

Mrs. Gerson turned to Mary. "See all the problems she makes for us! She doesn't do anything like she should. She just sits there dirty and crazy-looking. She doesn't belong here . . . I wish somebody would send her back to the hospital. She just doesn't care about a thing."

Shocked, Mary replied, "Oh. I'm sure she doesn't want to go back, . . ." and as Mrs. Gerson began to sputter an angry reply, Mary said to the postman, "Why don't you just give it all to me. I'll bring it to her. She's right there in the lobby."

Mrs. Redmont showed no interest in the mail. She made no effort to accept the proffered packet of postcards and circulars. Mary hesitated, then asked, "Shall I sort it out with you?"

Refusing to take the lack of response as a negative, Mary sat down beside the woman and began to handle the mail. She was quite surprised to find postcards from Austria, South America, Japan. She commented on one beautiful scenic card.

Mrs. Redmont looked at it and said, "That is from my old friend from Austria. Now she lives in Argentina. We both left the old country at the same time. We haven't seen each other for 36 years."

As Mary continued to comment on the postcards, she learned that Mrs. Redmont had lived in many lands, and had friends and family all over the world.

She picked up Mrs. Redmont's mail daily after this, and they would talk about some of it. Mrs. Redmont never opened the mail herself, but listened when Mary read it aloud to her. She never took the letters upstairs with her.

Mary learned a great deal about Mrs. Redmont during these talks. Especially that her husband had died while she herself was in the hospital . . . that she couldn't forgive herself for this . . . that she couldn't stand the lonely emptiness of her apartment . . . that she hated to eat alone and never cooked anything . . . that she wasn't taking the medicine that the doctor had prescribed when, at her insistence, he had discharged her from the hated hospital. It was sad to hear these things. Mary felt quite powerless as there was little she could do to change any of it.

But, each day, as she talked—Mrs. Redmont's blue eyes became a little less stark. Her drawn face softened. She seemed a little less remote.

Once, when Mary fumbled with the key to the outer door, Mrs. Redmont came and opened it from the inside. Mary's thanks were profuse. After that she needed no key. Mrs. Redmont opened the door each day. Mary continued the invitations to coffee—but Mrs. Redmont inevitably refused . . . politely, but firmly.

One morning, instead of inviting Mrs. Redmont into the office for coffee only to be refused, Mary brought two cups out to the lobby. The gesture was accepted, and the two ladies began to sip comfortably together. But very soon the telephone rang, and Mary ran in to answer it. Next morning, when she again brought the coffee out, Mrs. Redmont said, "Maybe, Mrs. Brenner, I'll come into your office with you so if the telephone rings, you won't have to run like yesterday."

She cares, she cares . . . Mary's heart hummed a lilt to her thoughts. She's not detached, she cares.

Now, each morning, Mrs. Redmont joined Mary in the office for breakfast. They added toast and jam to the coffee. Mrs. Redmont put on a little weight. One day, she wore a new blue dress. When Mary admired it, she told her it had been hanging in her closet since before her hospitalization, but this was the first time she'd put it on.

"It's just the right color for you," Mary told her, and was rewarded by a soft blush in Mrs. Redmont's pale face.

Since Mrs. Redmont was now in the office, and not in the lobby, the telephone complaints stopped. As the tenants drifted in for their bits of business, she would greet them since, having lived in the building for several years, she knew most of them by name. A little surprised at first, they began to respond. Sometimes, Mr. Farber, a lonely old gentleman from the seventh floor, would drop in, and Mary set up an informal afternoon teatime for them. She glowed with pleasure when the two old people left the office together. One sunny afternoon she saw them walking in front of the house. On the next rainy day, they chatted quietly together in the lobby

Over coffee, Mary told Mrs. Redmont that the doctor had urged her to take some pills, as she seemed a little poor-blooded. Mrs. Redmont said, "You should listen to him, Mrs. Brenner. You are a young woman. You need to keep your strength up."

"And you," Mary smiled back. "You should listen to your doctor. You need to keep your strength up too."

Mrs. Redmont didn't answer. The next day, when Mary hadn't brought her own pills, Mrs. Redmont said, "Why didn't you bring the pills, Mrs. Brenner? Bring them tomorrow—and don't forget them."

"I'll make a deal with you," Mary replied, "I'll bring mine and you bring yours. We'll remind each other . . . and we'll help each other to be healthy."

Although Mrs. Redmont didn't promise, the next day she produced, with a shy smile, an unopened bottle of pills. After that, the two women took their medication regularly, together.

Mrs. Redmont's appetite increased and her spirits rose. When Mary offered to take her to the beauty parlor to have her hair done for the spring holidays, Mrs. Redmont agreed. On her return, she collected more than one compliment from her neighbors.

It was just after the beauty parlor trip that Mrs. Gerson came into the office with a small brown package.

"This is for you," she said, handing it to Mary, "happy holiday."

"Oh, Mrs. Gerson, you shouldn't have. . . ."

"No, no," the clipped voice interrupted, "I have a reason. You are very nice to all of us . . . call up taxis in the rain . . . help with mail and bills. . . ."

"It's only my job," Mary said softly.

"Yes—and you do it very well. We are all glad you are here. We worried when Mrs. Bergson was leaving for awhile . . . but now, we hope you stay with us. This little gift is not for that . . . I brought it for you because you are so nice—so nice to Mrs. Redmont."

Almost in tears, Mary accepted the gift. Her ears echoed with the disdainful words of that first angry telephone call from this same lady, only a few months ago.

In May, Mrs. Bergson returned. She smiled "hello" to the pleasant-faced lady in the neat blue suit sitting in the lobby. Not until she walked into the office did she realize the woman's identity.

"Mary," she said, "What happened? I didn't recognize Mrs. Redmont."

Mary looked up from the typewriter and smiled at her boss.

"Welcome home, Mrs. Bergson," she said merrily, "don't you remember that you told me to be friendly with the tenants?"

Shura Saul

Excerpts from the Diary of a Social Worker

Anthony Pearl

First Visit, March 3

I arrive at Miss Camden's apartment about 1:25 P.M. It is very dark, as she has few lights on. The first thing I notice is that the entire place is badly in need of a paint job . . . paint peeling off the ceilings and just hanging there. The rooms are dull and dingy because the windows are quite dirty, and so are the blinds . . . some of them drawn more than halfway down the windows.

Miss C. is a small, white-haired, wispy little lady . . . she looks well over 75. Sad eyes . . . seems to have trouble breathing . . . pauses in her speech every few minutes to catch her breath (nervous or sick?). She seems fragile and very alone. There is something about her . . . an air of things long past. . . .

She shows me a letter from her landlord . . . that he expects to raise her rent because of some repairs he had made in the building. Miss C. feels it isn't justified because her apartment is in such disrepair. Just look at the sink and stove—both very old, almost ready to go—she tells me. She's had several rent increases in the past few years, she continues, but no new appliances and very poor service. Her total income is $162.80 per month (social security), and her rent is now $75. The raise would bring it almost to $80, which would be almost half her monthly income. I tell her about the rent increase exemption program for older people and promise to bring her the form later in the week.

Second Visit, March 10

After filling out the form, we sit and talk awhile. I notice a dog's dish in the kitchen and a leash hanging on the door and I ask her whether she has a dog. That was the wrong thing to do, I think, because she begins to cry and tells me how she had a dog who lived with her for 10 years, protected her, and kept her company. But the dog got sick and she had to call the ASPCA to come and put him to sleep. She used to walk him three times a day—she says—it gave her something to live for. Maybe I think she's crazy—she goes on—that the dog meant so much to her. People with families probably can't understand how much a dog means to someone like herself.

I tell her I understand. Has she thought about getting another dog? She has thought of it, but now, with her emphysema it is getting harder and harder to go for regular walks. It might be too hard for her to take care of a dog at this point.

I ask about friends . . . relatives. She hasn't seen her brothers in Connecticut for 20 years. She used to be a secretary in a law firm—but now all her old friends are dead. All but Joan, who married a wealthy man and lives out on the island somewhere. "Joan calls me sometimes," she says—but adds proudly "but Joan doesn't owe me anything."

"Neighbors?" I ask.

"Hardly anyone," she says. "The young couple upstairs are very sweet. One time, I was locked out of the apartment, and the young man climbed in through the fire escape. But who wants to bother young people? And why should any young people want to bother with me?"

Third Visit, March 24

Talked awhile with Miss Camden about how she spends her time. She likes to read but doesn't have a library card. She says the library is too far for her to walk to. I promise to help her get a senior citizen's card for transportation—then it would only cost her 30 cents to take the bus both ways. It would get her out of the house and off the block at least twice a month. She likes that. I'll also help her get the library card—and bring her some books for a starter. She likes that too.

I've been thinking about the puppy situation. How about a kitten? Cats are easier to care for . . . they are cleaner . . . and they can be fun too. That might be nice, she says . . . but where would she get one? I must look into that for next time.

As I leave, she asks me if I can bring some sewing thread and a pair of sharp scissors next week.

Fourth Visit, April 8

Miss Camden insists on paying for the scissors, saying that if I didn't take the money, she'd never be able to ask me again. She's right—and I take it. She seems to be looking and feeling a little better. Her hair is combed and she put on a bit of makeup. She's more cheerful too. Tells me that she's gone to the bank during the week and gotten her food stamp cards. Wants me to explain how to use them. I go over the procedure with her.

She's still breathing heavily, and I ask her when she's had her last medical checkup. I'm shocked to learn that she hasn't seen the doctor in six years . . . it's too expensive, she says, and she hasn't even tried to apply for Medicaid. I discuss it with her . . . tell her she should apply. She balks—doesn't want "charity" . . . too much red tape . . . all kinds of reasons. We talk and talk.

She shows me that she's trying to get the apartment to look a little better. She wanted the sharp scissors to cut and fix a piece of rug that the dog had chewed. She lets me fiddle with the TV, which was broken. I get it working, but it needs a few tubes, I think. She tells me she's called the landlord about the sink and stove. He's going to look into it.

She's been thinking about a kitten. It is a good idea, she says, I think I know someone whose cat had kittens.

Fifth Visit, April 20

Donna, the girl with the cat, came with me to deliver a little tiger-colored kitten. Miss Camden liked the kitten immediately, and named it Tiger —of course. At first, she spent a little time talking about her dog, recalling how much she loved him . . . but all the time the kitten is on her lap, purring away, and pretty soon, Miss C. goes to the kitchen, pours out some milk and feeds it.

A gap is filled. I can see how important it is to Miss Camden that this little thing will be dependent on her.

Sixth Visit, May 15

What a change in the apartment. The windows are sparkling and clean; the blinds have been removed and the sun is pouring in. The kitchen is scrubbed and the cracks in the wall filled. The paint is pulled down from the ceilings. Miss Camden tells me a man has worked there all day, and is coming back to paint.

She starts telling me how much she is enjoying the library books I brought her. She'll return them herself when she's finished reading. The kitten is jumping all over the place, and Miss C. is laughing. Her legs are full of scratches . . . but she doesn't mind . . . the kitten is a barrel of fun. I tell her she has to be more strict and train the kitten not to scratch.

Someone has called from the Medicaid office . . . they are processing the application but what a drag! It's going to take so long, and meanwhile, Miss C.'s breathing isn't getting any better. She says she doesn't care if she dies this summer, as long as her debts are paid. I say, "What about Tiger?" She says, "Well, yes, Tiger is important." She turns to the cat and says, "Go drink your milk, honey, drink your milk." After a few urgings the kitten actually obeyed. Miss C. is very proud and says, "She really understands me." Then she tells the kitten to "find the ball, Tiger" . . . and the kitten does that, too.

Miss C. turns to me and says, "If anything does happen to me, you'll see that Tiger is taken care of, won't you?"

I say I'd rather concentrate on seeing that she is taken care of . . . by making an appointment with the doctor even before her Medicaid comes through. She smiles at me and says she'll think about it . . . and "go along with you . . . always pushing me to do things I hadn't expected to do. . . ."

That's what I'm here for, I tell her with a grin. Well, we'll see what next week brings. Maybe she will agree to see a doctor!

The Man

As soon as Gina asked, "Where is Papa?" Mrs. Tomasino knew he had slipped into the bedroom again.

"Finish heating the sauce," she told her daughter, "and get the family to the table. I'll go to Papa."

Opening the bedroom door, she saw him sitting dejectedly looking out the window. When she looked at him, she was aware, as always, of that special heartbeat—"almost 55 years married," she would scold herself silently, "and you are still crazy about that man! You think you're still 16 years old, eh?"

She sat down beside him, reached for his hand. The strong, wide fingers were limp in hers.

"Carlo," she said softly, "again?"

He shook his head. "No, Maria, not again. Still. Still and always."

Alone together, they always lapsed into Italian. Although both of them had come to the United States as young people, they—like their families—had remained most comfortable with the old world language and ways of life.

"Ah, Carlo," she said, "We can still be happy."

"For what—happy," he retorted bitterly. "For growing old? For being driven . . . from my work, from my home? For what shall I be happy?"

"For each other," she pleaded. "For good health. For good children who love us and want us. For the sweet years we have shared. Who knows how many are left to us? Make it good, caro mio."

He pushed her away softly. "Nothing can be good," he said. "It is bad. It is wrong. My home is here, in this house, in this city. Here, where we made our life together. Everything here is mine . . . ours, Maria . . . we made it ours. Why should we leave it now?"

She looked at the handsome, angry face, the strong, leonine head framed in the ridge of white curls, the deeply lined cheeks, the sensuous, moustached mouth. She said nothing.

He waved his hand at her and turned back to the window. "Go," he said, "go to the table. I have a headache. I will not eat with you."

The family was already seated and waiting. As always, the sight of her offspring lifted Maria's spirits. She considered it quite an achievement to have borne and raised five healthy sons and daughters who, in turn, were raising bright and beautiful grandchildren. They weren't all here tonight, of course. Only Gina, her oldest daughter, her husband Tony, and their two teenaged children Antonio and Angelina were here, visiting from Boston. Sophia, her second daughter, had stopped in to say "hello" and share the evening meal.

"Where's Papa?" Angelina asked.

"Papa has a headache," Maria replied, slipping into her seat.

Gina said, "Again a headache. Every night this week, just when we come to visit, Papa feels sick."

"No," her mother said. "Not because you are visiting. You know that."

"What then?" demanded Antonio.

"Papa's heartsick," Maria told him gently. "He doesn't want to make the change."

"I know. I know," Tony interposed. "At his age it is hard to change."

Sophia interrupted. "You can't really know, Tony," she said. "You're a nice guy, but you can't really know how my father feels. Gina and I . . . we know." She turned to her sister. "Remember, Gina, when we were little, how he used to take us around 'his city' and show us 'his buildings, his bridges,' his work?"

Gina nodded. "Once he took us out to Queens. It's all built up now, but at that time it was like the country. He showed us this new drawbridge they were working on, and explained to us exactly how he planned the rock blasting so the water could flow properly."

"I remember too," Sophia said. "he called it 'his bridge.' He told us, 'see, little daughters, your papa helps to build the whole city. Not just one small bridge. Now boats will move down the river, cars will cross the river. This is a great city, New York.' "

"Oh, I remember something else that day," Gina said. "He said, 'let's go home now. I have a surprise for your mama.' "

"I don't remember that," Sophia said.

"You were too little, I guess. The boys weren't even born yet . . . no, mama was home with one baby. But I remember. You know what that surprise was?"

Antonio and Angelina, listening greedily, asked "What, mom?"

"It was this house," Gina said. "We had been living in a rented house. But when we came home that day, Papa said, 'Mama, I've been showing the girls our city. You know what, Mama? This is a good city. We should buy a piece of this city for ourselves.' "

Mrs. Tomasino laughed. "I'll never forget that!" she said. I said, "you crazy, Carlo? How we gonna buy a piece of the city? and papa said, 'a house, Mama. Our own house. With a garden. And plant a fig tree. And keep goats, to make cheese. Remember how your mama made cheese in the old country?' "

"A goat," Antonio asked excitedly. "Gramma, you had a goat?"

"Two goats," Gina told him, "until the city passed laws forbidding them. But we still have the fig tree. And gramma used to make cheese. Here in Brooklyn it was almost like the country."

Maria Tomasino looked at her grandchildren dreamily. "Ah, we had good times in this little house," she said, "Your Granpa, he always worked hard on his job. But never too tired, when he came home to do a little something in the garden. He loved this house. In the depression, he went without lunch, walked to work . . . sometimes across the bridge to Manhattan to save the carfare . . . always to be sure the mortgage was paid. The house was to be safe."

"When it was paid up," Sophia said, "Papa brought wine and we had a party. All the friends came. I remember Papa laughing . . . shaking hands."

"Yes," Gina chimed in, "Mr. Tossi, the boss, came. Papa gave him a drink and said, 'now Mr. Tossi, I got my own home.' And Mr. Tossi said, 'Carlo, congratulations.' "

Tony turned to his children. "You see, kids, this was like the family homestead . . . like an early American farmhouse . . . only it was here, in Brooklyn."

Antonio said, "It sure doesn't look anything like that now—with these tall buildings all around and the filthy streets."

Sophia replied, "It's not the way it looks that makes things so hard for Gramma and Papa. It's the changes in the people. . . ."

"The old neighbors moved away, I guess," Angelina said.

"Or died," her grandmother told her sadly. "Our new neighbors are strangers. Mostly young families, with small children. They don't talk Italian, or even English. They don't care much about two old Italian people in this little house with the only garden on the block."

"And muggings in the neighborhood," Gina said with a tremble in her voice. "Mama, do you know how we worry about you?"

"Yes . . . yes, I know," Maria said hastily.

Sophia looked at her suspiciously. "What do you mean, Mama," she said sharply, "I don't like the way you say 'yes, yes.' "

Maria turned to Angelina and said, "Angelina, how about a little more sphaghetti, carissima?"

"Mama," Sophia insisted, "you. . . ."

Gina interrupted. "I know, something happened and you didn't tell us."

Doggedly, they persisted until they dragged the story from her. Yes, Papa had already been mugged. By some miracle, he had mustered all his strength—old as he was—the assailant was young—to push the other man down and escape harm. The family was alarmed, reproachful.

Tony said, "You see how right we are. Mama, you must sell the house. Come live in the little apartment in our building. You will have everything you need. Privacy . . . a garden. It's clean. Safe. You'll have us nearby. We'll have you."

Gina leaned over to touch her husband's hand gratefully. "Mama, it is a good plan. Even if it does mean you have to move quite far away from here."

Her mother nodded. "It is a good idea. And you are good children. Don't you think your papa knows this too? You think because we are getting older we are losing our good sense? No, dear children,—he understands better than you."

"Sure, Mama, sure," Tony said, "that's why we think he should go along with the whole idea. . . ."

"Should—should," Sophia said passionately, "what does 'should' have to do with it?"

Tony retreated. "I didn't mean it that way," he told his sister-in-law. "I just want to make things better and I wish it weren't so hard on him to change."

Mrs. Tomasino interrupted them. She spoke slowly, gesturing with her hands as she shaped her words . . . as if she were touching her thoughts, moulding them for her family to see.

"Children. Listen. Your papa is like a tall, strong tree. He put his roots down deep, deep in this city. So many of them. His work, his home, his children. These are all roots. They tie him to his life . . . they nourish his life. A tree grows to the sky . . . a man grows to his future. Now it is here—his future. And it cannot be as he had planned it. Don't you see that? It cannot be as he planned it . . . and you want him to change . . ." she snapped her fingers . . . "like that!"

"No, Mama," Gina corrected her passionately. "We don't want. But it's got to be. We can't help it. He can't help it."

"Aha, now you said it, Gina." They all jumped at Papa's voice. They hadn't heard him come in. Knives and forks were stilled as the family turned to the commanding figure in the doorway.

"Yes, look at me," he said "Take a good look at your papa, Carlo Tomasino, the crew captain, the strong man. They told me 'Tomasino, now you are too old. Take it easy. You must retire.' Well, like you say, Gina, I cannot help that . . . it is the law. Then, the city builds tenements. I lose my neighborhood. Again. I cannot help it. I must give in. . . . I lose friends, neighbors. Some die. Some move away. I cannot help that either."

The voice grew fierce. "But I keep my own home. I keep my own home. This too I shall not control? How shall it be . . . not to decide where I live or where I die? No!"

The strong voice trailed into silence. He waved his arm almost helplessly and turned back to the bedroom.

Behind him, the door swung silently closed.

Maria flew after him. "Carlo, Carlo, I am afraid when you talk this way."

He sighed. "Maria . . . I shall have to give in, again and again. I don't think I can do it."

"Carlo," she replied, "Listen. To me you are always the man. To them, always the father."

He sat down suddenly. "Always?" he asked her. "How long is always, Maria?"

Shura Saul

The Schoolteacher

'I wish you'd get to know Mrs. Herzog," the administrator said to me about a month after I'd begun to work at the Home for the Aged Blind. "She's a retired schoolteacher. She's only been here a short time, and she's having a very hard time of it."

Mrs. Herzog turned out to be a white-haired little woman who held her head very erect and her eyes open. She didn't "look blind." She had heard of me, or rather, of the literary discussion group I led. She told me immediately, in a clear and definite voice, that she wasn't interested in joining the group, and she was understandably suspicious when I told her that wasn't the purpose of my visit.

"Then what do you want?" she asked, with more than a hint of hostility in her voice. "Everyone around here wants me to do something—and I just want to be left alone."

"I just want to get to know you," I told her. "I used to be a schoolteacher too."

This fact seemed to establish a bond, and she welcomed my visits several times a week. Each time I saw her, Mrs. Herzog went to great pains to be sure I understood that she did not belong in this place because she was so different from everyone else.

One day she told me, "Everyone here speaks with such an atrocious accent, sometimes I think I'll forget how to speak correctly myself. There's a woman at my table—do you know Mrs. Rose? You should hear her murder the King's English!" And she mimicked some of the speech she heard around her.

Another time, she said, "I was born in this country, you know. Everyone else here seems to have come from Europe. I'm a real American."

Still another time, "I was a schoolteacher, you know. The women here were either housewives or workers in factories or shops. I have nothing in common with any of them."

Mrs. Herzog looked forward to my visits, but she continued to remain aloof from everyone else. Through fall and winter, she was lonely, bitter, angry.

One of the most anticipated events at the Home was the Spring fashion show at which the members of the millinery group modeled the really beautiful hats that they had made themselves. This was an elegant affair attended by staff, residents, and relatives. The hats had been individually designed by our meticulous milliner and sewing teacher, Mrs. Ruby, who insisted on and taught quality sewing. Never having witnessed this legendary show, I asked Mrs. Ruby how the blind residents knew what was being modeled.

"I tell them," she said, "I describe each hat as it is shown."

"Would you mind," I asked her, "if Mrs. Herzog did some of that?"

"Beautiful," she answered, "but will she do it?"

During my next chat with Mrs. Herzog, I said, "Listen, I wonder if you'd give me a hand with something for the fashion show?"

Immediately, she became tense. "What," she asked in acid tones, "could I possibly do to help you?"

"Help me write the descriptive commentary," I suggested.

She snorted. "How can I do that? First of all, I can't see the hats. Then again, I can't see to write. And besides, who'd listen?"

For the first time in the months I'd been visiting with her, her reply didn't sound like a categorical refusal. I tried further.

"I'll help you," I said, "if you'll help me."

"How?" she challenged.

"Well, you can feel the hats and I'll tell you whatever you want to know and can't see. Then you dictate your description and I'll write exactly what you say."

She tested again.

"Why, in heaven's name should you go to all that trouble with me when you are perfectly capable of writing it yourself?"

I answered carefully. "Two reasons. For one, maybe you'd know better than a sighted person what to describe for other blind people."

"Well, maybe," she said, fencing with me. "What's the other reason?"

This was it. I knew that my answer would be crucial in her decision, and perhaps also, in our relationship. With a deep breath I took the risk.

"Mrs. Herzog," I said, "I want you to see how much I think you can contribute to our life here. I'm hoping that I can help you become a little more satisfied than you are now."

She didn't answer immediately. Her head went down and she pursed her lips. I waited. Had I gone too far, too fast? Well, if so, I had blown it.

Then she nodded. "You're honest," she said, "I can trust you. When do we start?"

. . . I can trust you, she had said. You won't "con" me . . . you won't kid me. You will make me neither more nor less than I am. . . .

Aloud, I told her, "Right now."

Facing each other across a small table we sat down with the hats, my pencil poised and ready. I picked up the first hat and described its shape, fabric, and color. Mrs. Herzog, rather nervously, dictated a description and I read it back to her. "This hat is a black felt cloche with a smart little brim to be worn over the eyes. On the left side there is a little veil held by a jeweled clip." A factual description, rather dull. Mrs. Herzog picked up the second hat.

After I told her the color, she asked, "Who made this hat?" I almost hesitated to read aloud the named pinned to the beret. It was "Mrs. Rose," and I had never forgotten Mrs. Herzog's ridicule of the lady. But the angry school-teacher was less angry now. She nodded at the name. "Oh, I know her. She sits at my table. Quite a sweet person, even though she doesn't speak English very well."

After a thoughtful moment she dictated her description. When I read it aloud to her, we were both startled. It read, "You see before you a beret. The cloth is velvet, the color gray. The sewing both precise and neat by Mrs. Rose. She's nice and sweet."

"Mrs. Herzog," I said with some excitement, "if I read this rhythmically, it's a verse. You've written a verse."

Mrs. Herzog closed her eyes and sighed. "Have I indeed," she said.

There was a long silence. What feelings and memories were racing through that proud head? Of the poems she had herself written at other times, in other places? Of verses she had helped the children compose? Of rhymes read aloud and judged after a school day? I never knew. I just held my breath and waited.

Finally, she groped for another hat on the table. "So, I've written a verse," she said in a tone I couldn't fathom. "Well, then, let's try for another."

The rhymes came pouring out . . . as if some fountain had suddenly been released—or some hidden wellspring tapped. Mrs. Herzog would ask me for the facts about the hats which she then combined with her own information about their creators. In true schoolteacher style, she had spent her first few weeks at the home learning the residents' names and personalities. From her mental records, she culled whatever complimentary comments she could design. Each verse, then, became a tribute to the milliner as well as to her work.

At the fashion show, Mrs. Herzog sat at the microphone with me. She had written an introductory verse which she memorized and recited herself. As I read each of the others, the lady modeling her own hat turned to Mrs. Herzog with a bow and a pleased "thank you" which rang through the room.

Of course, the verses were the highlight of the show. Mrs. Herzog concluded the affair, reciting humorously her closing verse.

> Now I'll put my verse upon the shelf
> And go and sew a hat myself!

The applause was almost thunderous. Mrs. Ruby was not one to wait. Immediately, she invited Mrs. Herzog to select cloth and join the sewing group.

But when Mrs. Herzog actually sat down to sew, she became impatient with her gnarled old fingers and her sightless eyes. She fought with the needle and thread, which doubled, knotted, and tore. Frustrated, she sat rigid with shame. She who had, in her day, taught hundreds of little girls how to sew! In that outraged moment she was helpless, defeated, trapped—trapped again by that damned blindness. She couldn't even leave the room, afraid to trip over a pair of unseen feet! But this was intolerable! She stood up, letting the hat form fall to the floor. Tearfully, unsteadily, she began to grope her way across the room.

"One moment, Mrs. Herzog," Mrs. Ruby called commandingly across the room. "I'll be right there."

She halted. Mrs. Ruby approached swiftly, kneeling a moment to pick up the hat. "What's the trouble?" she whispered to Mrs. Herzog.

"This is not for me," hissed the humiliated woman. "I can't sew anymore."

"Of course you can," said Mrs. Ruby. "Listen. The sewing needs a rhythm, just like your verses. Here," she helped Mrs. Herzog sit down again and placed a freshly threaded needle in her hand. "Listen to my beat and follow the pins along the seam. You can do it." Mrs. Ruby sat with her, beating a slow even tattoo as the faltering fingers found their way with the needle.

I'm not sure Mrs. Herzog ever really sewed very well in the home. But the conversations at the table, and the admiration of the other women were very important to her. That summer, she became the poet laureate, composing for every occasion and for anyone who asked. Children's birthdays, anniversaries, births of great-grandchildren—no one celebrated without one of her gay, brave little poems.

She no longer waited for me to come and do her writing. She learned to use a writing frame, and presented me weekly with her written material. As I read it aloud, she would dictate the corrections that had been simmering in her head all week.

The next year, our choral group was formed. The old schoolmarm undertook to teach the English lyrics to all the foreign-speaking ladies, Mrs. Rose among them. When we performed at a countywide spring concert, Mrs. Herzog's strong, sweet soprano rang high above the quavering old voices of her fellow choristers. Afterwards they marveled, "She has the voice of a young girl."

Then, one icy day of the third winter, I came to work and she was gone. She had been hospitalized for a viral infection and was very ill. Staff and residents all felt the emptiness of her absence. We visited her in the infirmary, only to find her unconscious and incontinent. "Well," we comforted each other, "80 is a ripe old age." And we began to prepare ourselves for her death.

Many weeks later, the doctor shouted over the telephone, "We've done for Mrs Herzog about all that physical medicine can do! Now get those group workers over here. If anyone can help her come back, they can."

I went quickly to the infirmary. She lay flushed and weak, but happy to see me. "I have a poem," she said, "it's been in my head for days, but I'm too weak to write it. Will you?"

Would I? I raced for a pencil.

After I left, the nurse telephoned to say, "Mrs Herzog hasn't had such a good day in a long time. Can you come again soon?"

I came every day, and so did others. And Mrs. Herzog did come back. A little weaker; a little thinner; a little less alert; a little more disabled. But she sang with the chorus. She wrote for the newspaper and, undaunted by her incontinence, she came with us on trips. We published two small volumes of her verses. One of these she illustrated herself with stick figures, for she was still learning to do new things.

A year later, she wrote a play in verse describing the routines of life in the home. It was the script for the first performance of the newly organized dramatic group.

When a resident council was finally formed, Mrs. Herzog was elected its first president.

And then, eight years after she had come to live with us, she died. Even in her death, she was creative. An innovator. In the past, funeral services had been held elsewhere and only a few residents were ever able to attend. Now, for the first time, administration and residents together held a memorial service at the home itself, so that all who wished might honor her.

Once a resident had said to me wistfully, bitterly, "Ah—what meaning does the life have here? When you die, you go out feet first—and not a word is spoken. It is as if you had never lived!"

Mrs. Herzog taught us another way.

Shura Saul

A Sketch

The nursing home for 30 women was a small, old private house that had been converted to its present use. It was crowded, but the matching spreads and curtains and scrubbed look atoned in part for the cracked walls and ceilings.

The very small sitting room was my work arena. Here I met with a group of ladies each morning in some mutually agreeable activity—current events, knitting, a "koffee klotch." We were flexible, unstructured, trying to build some friendly, normal human intercourse into the abnormality of institutional living. Here, where privacy was least attainable, we respected the privacy of each other's thoughts. Our mutual respect and kindness was sincere. In that room, together each morning, we were safe.

One day, I entered to find a new resident in the soft chair in the corner. Mrs. Cooper was a 75-year-old black woman who held her head proudly above her strong shoulders and well-shaped body. Her face was quite pretty —round and smooth for all her years. Her black hair was coiled in a neat bun. Her work-worn hands lay folded and relaxed in her lap. Only her feet, heavy and swollen, explained that it was very hard for her to get around.

Mrs. Cooper did not join our group. She sat quiet and removed in her corner, speaking with no one. Except for an occasional nurse's aide who might pop in for a moment, she was the only black person in the room. She looked, felt, and acted like "the outsider."

Her aloofness made the rest of us feel uncomfortable. Here we were, the white people, friendly and together . . . and there she sat, alone in her corner, the very stereotype of the segregated black person! We became increasingly distressed as she stubbornly refused to respond to our daily overtures.

When I talked this over with some of the nursing staff they told me, "Mrs. Cooper is a loner. She's not even very friendly with us, the black staff. She's cool with everyone."

Individual women in the group, sometimes crudely, sometimes with sensitivity, would comment to me about Mrs. Cooper's aloofness. To them all I said, "Someday, somehow, she will trust us enough to be friendly."

But I wasn't sure myself.

One morning, Mrs. Castiglione called out to her in broken English.

"Come here, Mrs. Cooper, we got room for you with us."

Mrs. Cooper only shook her head.

Mrs. Castiglione urged, "Come on . . . you hear us better. . . ."

Mrs. Cooper moved not an inch. Embarrassed, Mrs. Castiglione turned back to us with a mild shrug of her shoulders. We would all have to wait.

She watched us with great interest. I knew she was listening as she nodded, frowned, shook her head—all in appropriate response to our conversations and activities. Once, when we played some old-time songs, she hummed along, softly waving one unobtrusive finger in rhythm to the music.

Still, she remained in her corner . . . never communicating directly . . . never budging until an aide would come before lunch to help her back to her room.

But she began to soften. After many weeks she returned my smile with one of her own.

Sometime later, she answered me with a soft, "Good-morning." Not shy. Just soft. Each day I was permitted a few more words of conversation such as, "Isn't it a lovely morning?" or "That's a pretty dress you are wearing today." I would be rewarded with a pleased reply. One day, Mrs. Cooper volunteered that I was wearing pretty earrings. When I noticed that her ears were pierced, I bought her a similar pair. She wore them every day—and I realized that at least one barrier between us was removed. She was able to see me as a person now, a little better than before.

Still, she would not leave her corner to join us. I had to find a way to let her know she could trust us . . . but I really couldn't think of anything. I knew that words alone would not be enough. Something would have to occur —something, but what? What would get her to move, move over to the group?

Some months before Election Day, I set up a table in the middle of the small room and opened an "office" to register our residents for absentee voting. I invited Mrs. Cooper to sign up. She shook her head.

"No," she said, "I'll just sit right here. I'm not coming over there." (The table was less than five feet away!)

"Oh, come on, Mrs. Cooper," I coaxed. "It'll only take a few minutes to sign you up. Then you'll be able to vote in November."

'I'd like to vote," she said, "But I'm not coming to your table."

"How can I fill it out," I cried, "if you won't come here to sign up!"

She didn't reply. It was clear, that if I wanted Mrs. Cooper to register, I'd have to go to her. In that crowded room, I couldn't even move a chair! I needed something to lean on!

A little angry, but determined, I took a stiff notebook, went over and knelt beside her in the corner to take the necessary information. As I wrote in my clumsy position, I realized the room had grown suddenly quiet. Everyone in the room was watching. There I was, kneeling beside her chair, as Mrs. Cooper bent over me laboriously signing her name.

She hadn't moved—but she had done something! And I had met her more than halfway!

That incident was a turning point in our relationship. After that, she was more willing to let me know her a little better. She told me bits and pieces of her long life story.

She was born somewhere in the South. Her mother had been a child slave. Mrs. Cooper herself had come north in her youth, and had worked as a domestic and cook all her life. Her husband and sons (there had been five of them) had all been marginal workers. Hers had been the only income the family could ever really count on. Her husband had died almost 30 years ago. The boys had drifted, seeking work. She hadn't heard from them in a long time. Maybe they were dead. . . . dead too young, like their father. She told it all quite impassively—only the flash in her eyes revealed her feelings. She'd continued to work for white people. Sometimes she "lived in" . . . sometimes not. Occasoinally she told me a story about her work experiences . . . not much, just a small incident. She'd remember a kindness, a cruelty, an indignity.

Sometimes I felt she told me these stories just to communicate with me. Sometimes I thought she was testing my responses. Beneath her words I read the message that white people were not to be trusted . . . that white people exploited . . . did not respect . . . did not understand. And as accompaniment—her lifelong struggle to retain her dignity as she tried to fulfill her life needs. In her own way, she told me that she was a free soul. No one had ever owned her. No one ever would.

My whiteness was a barrier between us. But neither of us would, or could, change our color. Neither of us could atone for the deeds of others. We had to see each other for ourselves. Mrs. Cooper would have to see me as I was, just as she wanted to be seen by me.

We two would have to find a way to span the separations created by other people.

Some months went by. When the winter holiday season began, we planned gaieties around the house. Mrs. Cooper remained apart. Even Christmas was not to be shared with us.

Among the patients were a few Jewish women who felt "out of" these holiday festivities. Our group discussed this and, together, we planned a Chanukah party for the house. We learned new dimensions of this holiday— which were new to many of us who, because of the calender, had thought of it as a "substitute Christmas" for Jewish people.

We all found its theme of national freedom remarkably modern. Women of other nationalities recalled other such struggles. Some mentioned Garibaldi, others, the Church of England. The parallel with the modern black struggle was clear to us all.

As we talked and planned, I realized that Mrs. Cooper was, as usual, listening.

On the day of the party, the little room was more crowded than ever. There was a skit, some songs, small gifts. The Jewish ladies had advised that potato pancakes, "latkes," were a necessary refreshment. I had brought the makings and an electric frying pan which I had set up in the tiny isolation room across the hall. I put some oil in the pan and began frying. The first pancake smoked, sputtered, and fell apart.

My heart sank! I couldn't make the pancakes! I'd spoil the whole party! Just as I began to panic, a round black arm reached over from behind me and a soft voice whispered in my ear.

"Not enough grease in the pan, chile, your cakes will burn."

Mrs. Cooper eased me gently away, lowered herself into the small chair, and expertly fried the pancakes for the rest of the morning!

Shura Saul

An Open Letter to a Young Doctor

Dear Doctor,

This letter is by way of thanking you for your attention to a patient and, also, to ask you to consider further the subject on which we exchanged a very few words in the hall at the hospital, namely, old people and aging.

I watched you attend to your elderly male patient. I watched your skill. I appreciated the humor with which you accepted his angry retorts and his sheer cussedness. I admired the patience in your treatment of him, and I was grateful for your efforts to explain to him what he should and should not do. I realize that all of this behavior, on your part, reflects your skill as a doctor and your real caring about, and caring for, people.

Then, I thanked you in the hall and said, "The man is a free soul. He cannot bear to be restrained."

To which you replied that that might be so, but that the real problem was his disorientation which, you went on to assure me, was a consequence of and associated with his old age.

To this viewpoint I must take exception. Yes, this patient was somewhat confused as to time, place, etc. But I cannot accept this as a function of his age. To do so is to affirm a common stereotype of old people and aging: that is that old people must, by sheer virtue of their years, become confused and disoriented.

Doctors, psychiatrists, psychologists and others who have studied aging (with the same intensity and dedication that you studied medicine) have disputed this stereotype. I refer you to works published by the Group for the Advancement of Psychiatry (GAP), to works by Dr. Stanley Cath and Dr. Martin Berezin, material by Dr.

Robert Butler, Dr. Robert Fulson, Dr. Alvin Goldfarb, Bernard Kutner, Muriel Oberleder, N. W. Shock, and Simon and Epstein— to mention just a few. All of these experts suggest that *all* the circumstances of the person, rather than his age alone, are considerations in determining diagnosis and treatment.

Consider this patient you attended today. When he was 55, he underwent a prostate operation. He manifested much of the same behavior as today. He tore at the tubes, the dressings, raged and ranted, etc. No one attributed his behavior to his age, then. He was simply a very difficult patient!

This man's wife died 25 years ago, very suddenly. His response to this trauma was confusion, disorientation—to the point where he did not recognize his own children when he met them in the street. He was about 62 years old then—hardly old enough to be called "disoriented because of aging." Yet it took many months after his wife died for this man to pick up the threads of his life. He did— and held down a job, ran his own household, and took care of an invalid son for the next 24 years! He worked at his job until he was 80 years old.

Within the past 24 years, whenever this man became ill, he manifested the same confusion and behavior that he does now. Yet, he recovered, both physically and mentally, from several major episodes . . . at 72 from a serious attack of Menieres syndrome; at 80, and, again, at 82 from cardiac infarction. Tell me, at what point during these past 25 years was it correct to attribute his disoriented behavior to his agedness? At 62, when he lost his wife? At 70, at 80, at 82—each time during severe physical illness? Yet, each time, he recovered, and continued to function at a level that made younger people, observing him, say, "Wow, wotta man!" *At which point, then, doctor, would it have been accurate to have diagnosed his confusion as inevitable and, possibly, irreversible?*

One cannot know all such things about a patient one is treating. That is what makes it so dangerous to apply a stereotype . . . . a rigid, universalized concept that negates the quality of the individual and consigns him to a useless, meaningless generality! (This, we have all learned, is true of all stereotypes—isn't it?)

How about other aged people, aged 90 and over, whom I have known both personally and professionally, who underwent all kinds of surgery; cataract, mastectomy, surgery for cancer in various parts of the body, and who returned to their homes to live with no signs of disorientation at all? What does that do to the idea that "he's old, therefore he is disoriented." Or, "he is disoriented because he is getting old . . . . there comes a time. . . ."

I do not dispute the fact of your patient's current confusion. I submit merely that such a state cannot be attributed to the "inevitable consequences" of his aging process.

I suggest further, that those of us who serve, help, and care for people (doctors among us) need to understand older people. Before we can even do that, we must dispel the effects, on our thinking, of these unfounded and unscientific stereotypes of old people—especially those that suggest the inevitability and irreversibility of given states.

You are quite young, and I am middle-aged. Both of us, I think, want a chance to live and work for many years to come. Both of us will, I hope, reach a ripe old age and, perhaps, will need some kind of professional assistance. Neither of us would want our possible states of depression, confusion, and/or anger, which might conceivably manifest themselves in some form of unrealistic behavior, written off as consequences of our aging. Rather, we would want the professional's attention directed to the human condition and circumstances underlying our behavior in a stress situation. In fact, that is exactly what you (young) and I (middle-aged) want now from anyone who assists us!

There is no intention in this letter to criticize the quality of professional, medical attention that I witnessed given to your patient today. I do believe, however, that the attitude you expressed afterward about aging and disorientation may have a negative effect on a service you may give an old person someday. And I promise you that, unless it is eradicated, this same stereotyped view may well affect (negatively) some professional service to you and yours today and tomorrow.

I am sure that you are as unwilling for this to occur as I am.

Thank you again for your very kind attention, and please do think about this note.

Most sincerely,

Shura Saul, Ed. D.
Consultant on Aging

Young People Write of Aging

Young Hearts with Old Faces

Young hearts with old faces
Looking into a world of life
Knowing experiences that I may never understand
Carrying antique thoughts
In a bag of gold.

Young hearts with old faces
Seeing two worlds of hope
All their friends lost in times
I have never seen.
Crying over people who will never live again.

Young hearts with old faces are my treasures.

Jennifer Saul

Young People Discuss Aging

The teenage girls in this discussion were friendly visitors and recreation aides at a nursing home. This activity was part of a fieldwork program in a summer work camp. The discussion below is excerpted verbatim, and in context, from one of their interpretive seminars.

Voice. In the old age home, all the old people say, "I can't do it . . . when I was young, I did it." Like they were in a chorus, they keep on saying, "I can't do it."

Leader. How come?

Voice. Well . . . it's also because if we didn't go there they wouldn't be so pushed to doing things. Like that place doesn't have so many activities.

Leader. How come?

Voice. Staff at the OA home feel that these people aren't capable of doing anything at all.

Voice. They feel like they are going to die—they had their life.

Voice. I think they (old people) have fallen into a routine of the old age home. Like, you know, they don't have as many activities or things like that. They just sit around. So if there is a feeling that these people are old and they are senile, they can detect how you feel about them and they just grow right into the routine. They also feel like "Well, I'm old and senile and I can't do anything anyway."

Leader. How come?

Voice. A few of them I talked to say, like, "Now I'm old" and I feel like they have been pushed into a corner.

Leader. How come?

Voice. They think when they become old they become worthless. . . .

Leader. How come?

Voice. When a man gets to be 65, they fire him and hire someone young.

Leader. How come?

Voice. They have the impression when people get old, they get senile . . . even when they are not. They are afraid of becoming like that, old and senile, and so they push them into a corner like that.

Leader. You've given a lot of answers. When I said, "How come?" I didn't mean that you hadn't answered. There isn't just one answer to the points you've raised, and you've given several. You have said—people get old and tired themselves; you've said, younger people are afraid of growing old and push old people into a corner; you've also said, old people get a message abut themselves, that they are useless . . . and some of them seem to accept the message. Let's look at some parts of this social message to the aging person? What are some of them?

Voice. When you are 65 you can't work any more.

Leader. Do we agree that having to leave a job at any age can be a blow to a person? What else is happening to the older person when he has to retire?

Voices. Other things start happening.
They get poor.
They lose the chance to talk to people on the job.
You take pride in your work, and in yourself. You can lose that pride.
You might lose your identity.

Leader. When you work, you have relationships with people. You are open to new ideas and, you have a feeling of usefulness. In our society, work is a social as well as an economic role. OK . . . so there are many losses that occur a long with the loss of work role. What else might a person lose as he grows older?

Voices. You lose your friends. You have contact with death, because some of your friends die.
They could lose touch with reality . . . because the reality they knew isn't there anymore.

Leader. Instead of saying "they lose touch with reality," could we say that sometimes it seems to the older person that the "mat has been pulled out from under him?"

Voices. They lose their independence.
They resist change . . . the old person considers himself old-fashioned.

Leader. Do we also, sometimes, consider the old person old-fashioned?

Voices. Yes.

Leader. So it is not one-sided then. It's a two-way street. We must realize that how we consider the old person is also how he may consider himself. . . .

Voice. Another thing, I think is—like—when you get old you lose some of your senses. You can't see or hear as well. You get arthritis and you can't use your fingers. Even if you want to do things, sometimes you can't.

Leader. That's very important. There are physical changes in the body, and in perceptual capacities.

Voice. What about contacts with your own family?

Leader. What about them?

Voice. I noticed with my grandmother . . . she still does a lot of things . . . but when I talk to her, she doesn't seem to listen.

Voice. One old man in the nursing home talked to me about long hair and hippies . . . and I disagreed with him. He started to scream and yell at me and call me a dirty filthy commie and get out of his room and never come back. . . . I told him I would stay and we could change the subject—but he wouldn't accept me.

Leader. Do you think he acted that way because he is old?

Voice. I think he was scared.

Voice. I think he was probably like that all his life . . . probably when he was 30 he felt the same way—not because he's old.

Voice. My grandmother, she was over 80—she kept up with a lot of things and she was up to date. She was a very smart lady.

Voice. There's a lady in the old age home like that . . . her views are different from mine but she is really with it. That old man who yelled at you, its his feelings, not because he is old.

Voice. I want to say something. Some people don't get old. My grandmothers . . . when I wrote to them that I was working with old people, they wrote back. One said when I come home I have to teach her what I taught them because "I'm in their class." The other grandmother wrote back and said, "Just remember, I'm not in the same class as they are."

Leader. That's really great. Here are two different people and they have two different responses. That's the whole point we are making here . . . that people are different . . . and that old people are each different in their own way. When we understand this, then we can interact with them in a more reasonable way. It doesn't mean that old people are all right in their views, or all good . . . or all any *one* thing.

Voice. Does this have anything to do with old people falling into routines, like at the old age home. . . .

Leader. See. I'm asking you to think . . . not of "they" but of "him" and "her."

Voice. I was just going to say . . . if you just mention "old age home" some people will say something like "Oh—they're old . . . old people are all alike, . . ." and things like that, but at the old age home, each person is different, and that's what you learn from being there awhile. Because when you first get there you think that they all share the same problems. Some of their problems are the same, but each of them handles them differently.

Voice. It is like that. I consider each one of them as an individual.

Voice. I think we look at them for the stereotypes a lot, because we expect it. I was talking to one lady and she asked me if I believe in God, and I said no, and she said—oh you're a communist. And the thoughts began running through my head . . . this old lady . . . you know . . . and suddenly she began to laugh, she had looked at my face and she said, "I was kidding." Funniest thing, because I was ready to get defensive, and here she was kidding around. I had figured you know that she was old . . . the stereotype . . . and how am I going to explain to her. It was really funny.

Leader. Anyone else want to share something about a stereotpye?

Voice. The other day we were out on the porch and you know no one ever talks to each other. They just sit there and I said okay, the only way I'm going to get them into conversation is to ask a real controversial question. There were mostly women out there, and I tried to get them to interact. I explained about the women's lib movement and they all said, "Okay," you know, "if she wants to go out to work okay"—and I only ran into one woman who said woman's place is in the home. So like you know, it was strange, I was expecting them all to say, "What kind of a lousy mother is that? Running off and leaving her kids." And we were talking about what was bad and all that and they were pretty liberal and very far from the stereotyped idea of the old grouch sitting in the corner . . . with very right-wing views and everything.

Leader. Anybody else have something to share?

Voice. We had a discussion on youth and aging—and people in the senior citizens' center, they were talking to us. There were about 10 of us, and they were yelling at us—and they have a stereotype that all kids are bad and all teenagers are on drugs—but they didn't mean us, they—like—left us out of that class. They didn't know what we do and what we don't do, but just because we talk to them and we smiled they think we're not. . . .

Voice. "We're not talking about you. . . ." (Laughter)

Voice. Yeh, we get that all the time.

Voice. It's the same at the old age home, the kids here are nice, but those other kids . . . they're not. . . .

Leader. Wow—what does that tell you (Several voices, out of which emerges. . . .)

Voice. It's not only that, it's that we are the only outside ones who come in —we're the only people that they can relate to and that they see. . . . It's only that what they hear about and read in the newspaper is not the best thing in the world. So they think about the other kids and they group them. But then they see us, and it's just a tiny section of what they see outside and they just put us in that tiny section and they don't think there may be other people. . . .

Leader. Okay, okay what does that tell you about a stereotype? You say a stereotype is no good. How do you know that the stereotype isn't valid?

Voice. Well, you know by your experience . . . if you experience people and you have a stereotype about them . . . you see that it doesn't apply . . . then you know it's not right.

Voice. I think it's when you start realizing that all the people are really different, no two people that are really alike—you start looking at people as individuals and you realize that there really isn't a stereotype.

Leader. How does that jibe with what you were saying?

Voice. Because like—a lot of people—like—what they read in the newspaper is just like the business of the riots and everything, that's only one section. A lot of people classify all kids my age or a little bit older, if you have long hair so you're a hippie—and that's a stereotyped thing.

(Voices)

Voice. It's not real.

Voice. It's not valid either—it's a stereotype.

Voice. It's not that it is a stereotype—it is a generalization.

(Excited jumble of voices—some voice rises)

Like I was talking to this one lady, and we were talking about how people just generalize—she's very aware and very perceptive—and you really can talk to her. She felt bad because the way these people, they take one incident and the way they generalize, and they say, oh look, it's happening all over and it's a group of people. Then I talk to this other lady, and she happens to be very, very prejudiced—and she just says that all the black are all bad no matter what. I was going to try to explain to her but she has the wrong idea about things . . . that there are white people who are just as bad but she just wouldn't listen, she just said no, and she would get angry at me.

Voice. Well, it's very strange, some of them just don't listen and they don't realize that all people are different.

Voice. I'm not denying that there are stereotypes. I know there are.

Leader. There's a concept of a stereotype, is that what you're saying? There's a concept that this is what a teenager is, this is what an old person is, etc. I think that what is also being said here is that once you get to know a person, the stereotype becomes an abstraction, a generalization, which does not necessarily apply to the individual.

Voice. That's really true . . . I was talking to a woman yesterday and she said to me, all the young people here are so respectful to me, I don't understand where are all the teenagers they talk about who are disrespectful? I don't see them, where are they? (Laughter)

Voice. I think that stereotypes mean a lot because they don't give people a chance to find out what others are really like.

Leader. Yes, there's no question about that.

Voice. They mean so much because they tell you why some people never take the time to find out what's below the stereotype. The outside appearance . . . doesn't necessarily tell you what's deep inside them.
(General jumble of "right, right")

Voice. I think we could say not everybody believes in a stereotype. How can you stereotype a whole set of people? That's why we are taking the time to get to know people as individuals, and not only as a group.

Leader. Okay—let's just recapitulate. Groups have stereotypes of other groups until they begin to have some experiences, along with some interpretation of these experiences . . . can you buy that idea now?

Voices. Yes . . . Yes.

Leader. Now, remember what we said before . . . about this personality which gets all these outside messages to the effect that he's not good enough for this or that . . . his body also gives this message . . . you're not well enough to do this or that . . . what happens to him?

Voice. I think he will begin to withdraw within himself because all these things that are happening around him are like hurts. You know, they hurt him and when something hurts you . . . sometimes . . . you just "go into yourself" to coin a phrase.

Leader. When something hurts you, what do you do?

Voice. You build a wall.

Voice. You protect yourself.

Voice. It depends on the person.

Voice. Some will feel depressed.

Voice. Some get defensive and build a little shell.

Voice. It's all a type of defense . . . what they're doing . . . whether you're removing yourself . . . or you're not listening . . . it's serious . . . you're building a wall around yourself.

Leader. Could we say that the person who hears this message, begins to feel all his supports being withdrawn . . . in order to defend himself against being told how weak and unimportant he is . . . such a person sometimes begins to withdraw into his shell. He begins, if you please, to accept the stereotype about himself? Is this possible?

Voices. Yes . . . Yes.

Leader. We talk about "society and environment shaping the individual" . . . this is one way it happens. Just as you have described it.

Link to My Roots

A Student

Ever since I was a young child I can remember having had a special relationship with my grandmother. Both my parents work and when I was small my grandmother cared for me during the day. Through the years I think that the relationship has changed . . . we have both grown older and I think that we both observe and perceive things differently.

She has been a close personal link to the past for me. Her tales of early life in Europe have had a strong effect on me and sometimes I can identify with her experiences.

Although she is physically a strong woman, emotional changes have made her increasingly dependent on my family. She undergoes cyclical periods of depression and, therefore, resides with my parents periodically throughout the year. I remember how I would come home from high school to find her sitting on the couch with a sad and hopeless look on her face. I would talk to her and try to get her to come for a short walk, looking for something to involve and activate her. I remember the mornings. They were the hardest . . . just to get her out of bed when all she could say was "I can't."

It would seem like a miracle . . . the morning she would awaken with great excitement wanting to do everything at once as if she were releasing months of untapped and stagnant energy.

Our relationship has been a close one. Both of us, at different stages in our lives, have been dependent on one another in different ways.

I have a strong emphathic feeling for her. Sometimes I think that I can feel from looking into her eyes what she is experiencing. I have tremendous respect for her; especially for her strengths and weaknesses . . . the ways she has coped with the many changes and crises in her life. Sometimes I see parts of her personality in me. She has helped me to gain insight and to widen my perceptive dimensions in different ways. She has shown me two worlds . . . the strong roots in the old world with its tempo and wisdom often far ahead of the new. She has helped me to realize the richness of experience.

Two Clients

Nelson Burros

Helping is often a more complicated and extended act than I had ever thought it to be. Let me recount a working experience with two older women welfare clients of mine.

The women were Mrs. Heller and Mrs. Shalin. They live in a large apartment house in an area adjacent to Harlem, but with a different character because of the large numbers of elderly Central and East European emigres.

Mrs. Heller, the primary tenant, was a 65-year old woman, born in Europe of Russian-Jewish working-class parents. She had a serious physical limitation as she was legally blind. She also suffered from an arthritic condition that made it difficult for her to do her housework. Despite these problems, she seemed very enthusiastic about being alive, and was active to the utmost limits of her capacity. The house was filled with plants that she had been growing for many years. She tried to keep up with the news of all the world through her radio, now that she could no longer read. More important than any of these details was her philosophy that life is precious and to be lived as fully as possible.

On the other hand, Mrs. Shalin was an 80-year-old woman descended from the Russian aristocracy. Born the daughter of a provincial governor, she had married a count who was a vice-admiral in the Czar's army. She had had a fascinating life story, which could be the stuff of history books. Since 1950, she had been renting a room from Mrs. Heller. Mrs. Shalin, too, suffered from illnesses that limited her activity but, unlike her landlady, she only looked forward to dying. Her attitude toward life seemed to be the opposite of Mrs. Heller's. Being alive was a burden to be carried begrudgingly until death removed the weight. It was not so much that an afterlife would be so heavenly, but that this life was so painful and hellish.

The two women had an interesting relationship. Mrs. Shalin treated almost everyone, including Mrs. Heller, with aristocratic disdain as though she were still the countess surrounded by servants and respectful subjects. Mrs. Heller seemed to have been able to accept these mannerisms without becoming subjugated, without losing her temper, and yet managing to do those things for Mrs. Shalin that were necessary to her well-being. Watching them together was like watching a sort of ballet, performed by faltering dancers whose stumbling efforts might bring tears to the eye, except that their intentness and earnestness provoked a growing recognition and pride in their performance.

My initial contact with these clients occurred through a regularly sched-

uled visit once every six months. At that time, my major concern was to se-
cure a partial housekeeping allowance for Mrs. Heller, who no longer felt
strong enough to do the heavy cleaning. I was impressed and affected by
these ladies. They were interesting people with remarkable personalities,
whose fascinating experiences and histories I enjoyed hearing. They enjoyed
talking with me, sharing their experiences, feelings, and complaints. I also
seemed to inspire maternal or family feelings within them, especially within
Mrs. Shalin. She seemed to accept me as an equal; someone who could understand her; someone whom she couldn't order about, who wouldn't permit her
to do so.

This stable living situation was swiftly shattered, shortly after my second
visit, by the sudden death of Mrs. Heller who, one night, was rushed to the
hospital only to die very early the next morning. The irony of this event was
almost unbearable. The independent person, full of life and wanting to live
—she dies. The dependent person, wishing only to die—she lives on.

I was alerted to Mrs. Heller's death by calls from neighbors. Later the
same day, I was informed that Mrs. Shalin's doctor felt that it was vitally important for her to enter a hospital for necessary medical care. He considerel
her unable to care for herself without Mrs. Heller. No other alternative was
suggested for providing medical care for my client. And I was the one to arrange for her to enter the hospital.

What was supposed to take a few hours to arrange took more than a
week of frustrating struggle, and the question, later on, would be: "For what
purpose?" For Mrs. Shalin did not want to go to any hospital. She wanted to
die in her own house, in her own bed. She and I talked. We discussed. We
argued. . . . I even tried to use what I knew of her religious values to argue
that she had no right to usurp God's prerogative concerning the disposal of
her life. But to no avail. She might not order me about, but neither would she
do anything that she did not want to do.

The second day I visited her, she reluctantly agreed to go to the hospital,
and I called for an ambulance. But by the time the attendant and policemen
arrived, she had changed her mind with the "help" of a couple of suspicious
neighbors. After it had become clear that Mrs. Shalin might prolong her stay
at home for a long time, I worked out a makeshift arrangement with several
neighbors to visit her several times a day to provide food, medical, and
housekeeping services. This arrangement involved not only scheduling but
also mollifying her neighbors throughout the rest of the week. For Mrs. Shalin's aristocratic and overbearing manner had a predictably alienating effect on
them, particularly since her German-Jewish neighbors felt they were helping
her only out of human charity and their high regard for the late Mrs. Heller.

On the third day of this sequence, Mrs. Shalin presented me with a gift
of a bottle of sauterne wine in appreciation of everything I had been trying to

do for her. In the midst of the mutual frustrations and our own kinds of despair, there was evidence of the mutual respect and liking that we had for each other. It was as though every human scene, no matter how sad and depressing, is touched with human warmth.

At the beginning of the second week, Mrs. Shalin became so physically uncomfortable that she agreed to enter a hospital. After I called the hospital for an ambulance, I telephoned her neighbors to help her get washed and properly dressed to receive her medical guests. Ah, such pride! Unfortunately, by the time I could get to her building, she had already been picked up. I was not to talk with her, nor see her alive again.

During the next three weeks, while she was in the hospital, I did not have an opportunity to see her as I was quite busy with the 59 other cases on my welfare load of 60. I also must have felt that everything would be as all right as possible, now that she was where she was supposed to be.

Then one afternoon, I received a call from one of her friends who told me that my client was receiving very inadequate treatment at the hospital. Mrs. Shalin had again managed to alienate the medical and nursing staff with her overbearing manner. Thus the nurses and the aides did not want to have anything to do with her. This friend had also complained but to no avail. As a result, Mrs. Shalin, who was incontinent, often lay in wet, damp sheets for several hours before a nurse would change them or until a friend would come to visit.

The next morning, before I could get to the hospital, this woman called again to tell me that Mrs. Shalin had died during the night. Later that day I called the social worker for that ward. She admitted that the hospital was so understaffed that there was a tendency for the staff to neglect those patients with the least chance to survive. This staffing problem must have reinforced the effect of the alienation that Mrs. Shalin inspired. The social worker told me that this situation was tragic, but she felt that there was little that could be done until the hospital could hire more staff.

At first, along with my sadness, I was absorbed in my own sense of guilt for having deserted Mrs. Shalin once I had had her admitted into the hospital. I kept thinking of what I might have done . . . for example, I should have alerted the hospital social worker to prepare the medical staff for her behavior so that it would not have had such a disabling effect.

Later, I realized with anger that I had been a blind messenger for a system which decreed only one choice for this sick, older person . . . but which failed to offer anything like adequate facilities and resources to make that choice a responsible one.

When I Think of Old People

Leslie Hall

In June, 1962, I was put on a jet by my parents and flew with my brother to St. Louis. This was our summer vacation. We were to visit our great aunts and great grandmother. We were met at the St. Louis airport by my grandparents and great aunt. They drove us to our great grandmother's house where we were to live for the summer.

We went up to her room to see her. She was about 93 at that time. We walked into her room and saw an old, wrinkled, tiny lady on a bed. All she could do was move her right arm and turn her head enough to see out the window to her backyard. She was totally paralyzed otherwise. We both kissed her "hello," and she started crying. At that time I couldn't understand why, but now I really think that she was very happy that she had someone there who was young whom she could watch and with whom she could talk.

Each night that summer I went to bed thinking that when we woke up she would be dead. I was 10 that summer and it was the first time I really thought about being old. From then on I always related being old to death.

The summer of 1969 my great aunt came to visit us. She was 86. She shared my room with me. Each morning I would look at her. Each morning she would lie very still with her eyes closed. I would be afraid each morning that she was dead.

I am very afraid now of being very close to or living with an extremely old person. I have never experienced the death of anyone in my family, and I know it will have to come.

A month ago, I received a letter from my great aunt. Her brother had just died. He was in his sixties. She wrote how surprised she was that he had died first. She had always expected to die first.

Now, when I think of old people, I think of dying.

An Experience with a Senior Citizen

Harriet Gribben

I met Mrs. Parks when I was in college, probably in my sophomore or junior year. Mrs. Parks lived in the community and would attend many of the lectures, meetings, demonstrations that were held on the campus. She was rather quiet when I was first introduced to her, but she had already made contact with some of the campus activists, and was always eager to meet new people.

Through discussions with Mrs. Parks, we learned that she had been a nurse and about the difficulties she had encountered in pursuing this as a goal. Now, she would say, with humor, that it helped her take care of her husband who was rather ill, and she could also patch up, or offer advice, to her young friends. Mrs. Parks was a fervent socialist and has been politically active all her life. She felt that now she was retired, she had more time to take part in peace and antiracist activities. She was extremely active in Women's Strike for Peace and would come to campus with a petition, leaflets, and buttons.

By the time I was a senior, Mrs. Parks was well-known to and close to a group of us. She would often take part in our meetings, and was interested in us as people—what we would do when we graduated, who was dating whom, an so on. She would also urge everyone to continue struggling. She told us we would grow discouraged as she had many times in her life but she knew she must work for change for the rest of her life and she knew we would, too. She would understand our happiness at involving other students. (She gave several of our "recruits" a subscription to a radical newspaper as a graduation present.) Mrs. Parks often felt sad that her meagre strength would not allow her to picket, and the like, but when there was a successful student strike in October 1967, she came to the campus with a shopping cart full of cookies to help us along.

I think what I found so rewarding about my relationship with Mrs. Parks was her presentation of a really positive image of an older person. Certainly, she was somewhat of a "ham," after she felt comfortable with us—she loved making speeches or posing for pictures. She was a little forgetful and sometimes didn't listen too well. But my basic image of her is of a woman who did not allow adversity, or failing health or discouragement, to stop her. It troubled me (before and after meeting Mrs. Parks) to hear so many of the older people I know being so conservative in their views; to hear people of my parents' generation telling me that when I get a little older, my ideas will change, or I won't have time to be involved. Mrs. Parks is somewhat of a negation of all these attitudes. It gives one a whole new perception on aging in the sense that she has refused to be stereotyped into any role. She has had thes strength of conviction to continue working. Her great respect for the young also has fostered a reciprocal respect for older people.

The relationship between the students and Mrs. Parks was, of course, really beneficial to both. We benefited from seeing her as a sort of model for ourselves, and because we knew she enjoyed being with us. Mrs. Parks derived much satisfaction from being included in our activities and being respected for her knowledge and activities.

Since graduating from college, I don't see Mrs. Parks as often, but I have run into her at a meeting or on the avenue with a petition. One final note must be added. When I got married, Mrs. Parks insisted on giving us a gift. She gave us a glass bottle that she had brought with her from Europe. Enclosed with the gift was a card stating that she was like the old woman who lived in a shoe—she had so many children she couldn't always remember their names but did love us.

Old People Write of Aging

Getting Older . . . Older . . . Old

You don't get old all at once. You notice the first wrinkle, the first gray hair . . . but you are too busy living to really think of "when you'll be old."

Then, one day, you are "over 75!" Out of habit, you continue doing all the things you did all your life.

You take care of your husband with constant concern for his health and well-being. (I am fortunate to have a husband who is a great comfort and help to me in all ways, even in the process of becoming, and being, old.)

You keep house—with more effort, of course.

You still do little things for those around you.

You also do your small share toward peace and a better world.

You anxiously watch the progress of your children and grandchildren—and hope that they will have a better life in a world at peace and real brotherhood.

127

You think of the past, and you are sorry for all the wrong things you did. You regret not to have done more of the right things.

You long for all the dear ones who have gone.

You cherish the ones still around and want to see more often.

You try not to "push time" unless a dear one is ill or you have a sleepless night.

You plan for tomorrow . . . next year . . . and next . . .

And you know that there are not many of those left for you at your age so you feel a little sad!

●–●

Rose Rudin

How an Eighty-three Year Old Man Looks at Life

Froim Camenir

My few words on this topic will not be a resume for all old people because each one of us looks differently at life. I'll describe my own view of life.

Since elderly people die before younger ones, I do not worry about death. Since death comes "willy-nilly" I am not sure of tomorrow's day—so I appreciate every day of my life. I regard each, not as the forerunner of my tomorrow's day of death but, rather, as the continuation of my yesterday of life. Like any other day, it is welcomed because it brings life, pleasure, and the power to think.

My daily routine as an 83-year-old man (except for a change in the quantity of physical work) is no different from when I was age 73, or 63, or 53. It is true that, physically, the body becomes weaker, and we cannot perform the work or activities that we could in our younger days. Personally, however, I am in quite fair physical condition.

Some elderly people are afraid of death. I am not. Death is another form of existence, which is not known to us, I am not a religious person—however, I think that some sayings in the holy scriptures are correct—for example,

"From dust thou cometh to dust returneth." I surely do not believe in resurrection!

A number of philosophers have discussed life and death. Some have praised the stage of youth—"De Juventute." Some have praised the stage of old age—"De Senectute." Leo Tolstoi wrote a nice little story about death, called "The Three Deaths." He describes the death of a rich, capricious old lady who dies in the middle of a journey between Moscow and the Crimea; the death of an old driver dying peacefully on an old peasant oven; and the death of a tree that is cut down to become a cross on the grave of the old driver. It all takes place early at dawn, a beautiful description!

However, I do not always think of death. Since I am an optimist by nature, and since death is not such a pleasant topic, I think mostly of life's problems, which we each face. I do not work any longer in my profession, so I don't have to think about earning a living. I am the secretary for a few fraternal organizations so I am quite busy with some actual secretarial work. I am also always thinking of ways to improve our work there. It is quite a problem to maintain these groups because I deal with old people who are faced with many problems such as health, income (most of which is based on social security payments or union retirement pensions), and family relationships.

Of course, I think about my family. How will my wife feel when I die? (She is quite a bit younger than I.) I think of my only daughter and her husband, who drive about in their cars daily. I am concerned about possible accidents. I think of my grandchildren and hope that they will be able to keep their various jobs.

I read in the newspaper how many teachers, engineers, and others are being fired. I think of the unhappy people (unemployed in many states) and how they could be helped. It breaks my heart to see the condition of our country, which has come to such a state that our "almighty dollar" has fallen so low on the international exchange. When I came to this glorious country in 1913, carfare was 5 cents with two transfers; the price of a letter only 2 cents, a postcard was a penny; the best meat was 35 cents a pound; a pound of bread was 8 cents. These concerns cause me to think about other serious social conditions—such as a person being afraid to go out alone in the street at night.

I think of the ignorance of many of our people, so many of our legislators who allow this unnecessary war in Vietnam. Our young boys die for nothing, tens of thousands dead and injured . . . billions of dollars spent and the question arises: "Why all these losses? In the name of what?" It seems that it is easier to ask the question than to get a logical, reasonable answer—and I, as an old man, am shedding silent tears, helpless to do anything to change the situation.

The only consolation I do have is to see the protests of our young generation. Their work, their protests follow the work of my generation. We taught them to work toward a better life without wars and without unemployment.

I am glad, and proud, that members of my generation were actually instrumental in achieving unemployment insurance, social security, teaching and enlightening the younger generation about the structure of our society, about minority groups.

All in all, old people play an important role. We are consumers, which is good for the economy. We are a political power—through our millions of votes we can elect a government more sensitive to our needs and the needs of all people.

We can offer support and guidance to the young generation. There are quite a few youngsters in my own family—nephews, grandchildren, nieces—who always ask me about my life, my studies, my teachers—in general, about the customs and life of my young days. They are interested in knowing what my world was like when I was young.

Some old people who are scientists, musicians, doctors, lawyers, actors, do still practice their professions, and the young generation can learn a great deal from them.

When this 83-year-old man gets up in the morning, he observes the sky is blue; the trees and grass are green; the sun shines; the birds sing; the city is in motion; people (most of the time) work and are happy. Children of all ages attract my attention. I see them grow nicely, strong. I believe they are willing and anxious to learn from the old generation—and the old generation is only too glad, happy, and also anxious to give to them.

This is the way I, an 83-year-old man, look at life.

Old Parents

For reasons we could not control
This Home has now become our home,
We may not live amongst our own
We who are blind and aged grown.

Our children must their own lives lead,
Their own tasks do; their own times need.
Here we live in calm and rest—
Indeed, for us, this is the best.

To God nor man bemoan our fate
But join in friendship; cast out hate.
Let peaceful living be our goal
As befits a human soul.

(Translated by Shura Saul from Yiddish Verse Written by an 83-Year-Old Resident of a Home for Aged People)

My Advancing Years

Frieda Laufgraben

My advancing years? Very much like my early years!

Curiosity and involvement have been part of me as long as I can remember.

I think a good starting point would be at the age of 54 when a piece in *The New York Times* attracted my attention. "The Academy of Medicine would have an all-day seminar on the need for Licensed Practical Nurses."

I attended, became carried away with the idea, and enrolled for the one-year intensive course, but was met with humorous harassment from my family and close friends.

Back to discipline and study at the YWCA and clinical practice and training at Beth El Hospital, now known as Brookdale. It was definitely one of my roughest years, but without the cooperation of my husband. I know I could not have done it! He relieved me of almost all the family chores for that year.

Seven weeks before graduation I very suddenly found myself a widow!

My impulse was to drop nursing, but with the encouragement of my instructors and director of nursing, I completed my course. "You have so much to give," is what they insisted.

Shortly after, the State Board Exams came up and still in my dark hours, I was shocked to learn that I came through with 93 percent. This was my green light that I must carry on.

I worked at Maimonides for about 10 years on a per diem basis only so that I could continue to maintain contact with my family, friends, and community.

I continued my membership in two organizations, always in some active capacity, including the presidency of Kings County Jewish Veterans, Ladies Auxiliary. This consisted of 30 auxiliaries—over 2500 members.

At present, 15 years later, I am president of the Friendship Club, over 300 members, serving on several committees, and the nearest thing to my heart is the NRA (Neighborhood Resources for the Aging).

Not at all easy! Many mornings it would be so nice to stay in bed—a pain here, an ache there, but with a little struggle, get the curlers in the hair, dress slowly, put the lipstick on, and miraculously you're ready to go!

I'm satisfied with small daily blessings and with helping one person if I can.

A regimen, conducive to good health, is worth trying.

I have worked for six summers as a nurse in children's camps—work four days each year on the Board of Elections—took a 31-day trip abroad, occasional shorter trips, weekends with family or friends, their homes or mine, and manage to squeeze in a luncheon, book review, a bit of reading and knitting, and a weekly game of Canasta.

Yes, I do my own housework and enjoy my own cooking. Actually there is always "something to do."

My thanks to my personal friends and family, especially my grandchildren who understand when Grandma is busy.

On Being Involved

Pauline Affronti

When I was young my involvements were mostly being a wife and mother. It was a very happy involvement. But time passes so quickly, and soon the family has grown and left home, and then you're left with just your husband. It also comes to pass that he has gone and I'm left alone.

I felt so sad and lonely for awhile until my son insisted I take a trip cross country to California by bus. I had traveled plenty with my husband, and my son said I should continue, so I did. I didn't know a soul on the bus, but soon we became one big happy family. By the time I got back home I began to realize that I had to be with people. Thank God, I'm an outgoing person. Soon I joined the AARP and heard about a club being started for Senior Citizens in Maimonides so I became involved.

My whole life and being became exciting to me again. I started with people, with older adults, and enjoying it very much, soon I became president of this club. For two years I was very active with the club and outside activities, that never did I have a chance to think in terms of loneliness and sadness.

Any person who feels lonely when left alone, man or woman, should join an organization with their age group and become involved. It is the most rewarding thing that can happen.

Growing old? Never! Moving around makes you feel younger, look younger, and even eases health problems.

Part III
Background Discussions

"Omniconvergence"

The vignettes describe some real experiences and circumstances of people growing old in today's world. These individuals' concerns have stemmed from their individual life circumstances, from changes related to their senescence, and from the world around them.

The construct of "omniconvergence," developed by Dr. Stanley H. Cath, suggests a useful, integrated approach to all these factors. He writes:

> "For ease of communication and conceptualization, a new topographical and dynamic psychological construct is useful—omniconvergence (or "omnicon"). This term includes not only phenomena in the personality structure (ego, superego and id) but also in the physical structure of the organism (the body and the body ego) and the socio-economic, ethical and purposeful environment. Omnicon thus signifies that the total human being and his personal cosmos are involved in the various epigenetic phases of loss of self and others. . . The ego's attempts at restorative processes will best be understood when seen in this total perspective of multiple converging epigenetic variables, and we are thus spared from taking sides in what appears to be a re-creation of the conflict between theories on the significant external and internal factors."[1]

This concept underpins a flexible approach to service and education for service to older people.

Some Implications for Service

The older person, like any other, is helped best when he is perceived as an individual with a life-style and integrity of his own. Help is given and received best when it is offered in harmony with the personality of the individual, family, or group of people, to be helped.

Any offer of service, or help, is an expression of human relationship, a bridge between people. The essence of this relationship is the affirmation of a human commonality, the acceptance of a broad, basic wellspring of humanity to which each person can refer, from which each may draw, and which grants the right to one human being to help another. The giver and the receiver are at the two ends of the bridge. The content and context of the service are the bridge. The helping agent must know all three components; himself, his service and its context, and his recipient.

To know oneself is to have self-awareness within a given situation. The donor of the service must accept the possibility that some of the myths and stereotypes about aging might be influencing him and that he may be unaware of their influence. The stereotype often masquerades as a "good intention," may stem from well-meaning ignorance, and always affects the appropriateness and fruitfulness of the service relationship. Self-awareness is a first step toward eradicating the effects of a stereotype.

The next step is to assess the individual situation, to understand its underlying dimensions and to know and review alternatives. It is important to see the realities and possibilities of a situation as well as its limitations. *Practical considerations* are usually clear: what size, how much, when, and so forth. More subtle are the *emotional dimensions* that affect behavior and become very real factors in the service exchange. *People's feelings*, therefore, become real and practical considerations for the service worker.

FOR EXAMPLE. At a rehab center, a physiotherapist was teaching an 80-year-old, post-stroke woman to walk. The son observed his aged mother's struggles and stopped the treatment saying, "Don't torment my mother." He insisted on discontinuing the service as he found his mother's condition unacceptable to himself. His feelings were interfering with the process of helping his mother recover some of her independent functioning. The total treatment team (nurse, social worker, physiotherapist, and other workers at the center) met with the son and explained the service and its process. They gave him a chance to review his feelings in light of a new understanding. After this, he gave his consent. Treatment was resumed, and his mother did begin to walk.

Another consideration demanding the worker's attention is the *expectation* of the service-recipient.. This generally derives from his perception of the worker's role, which may be quite different from the worker's own ideas. Much misunderstanding can develop from such a discrepancy in expectations and views. This can happen when *communication* is not explicit. The person who offers help must be clear about what he can or cannot do and must explain and clarify the limitations as well as the possibilities of his services. He must also enable the recipient to express his ideas about what services he needs and desires. Only when this communication is clear, can the prospective recipient decide whether or not to use the service. Such clarification is primarily the worker's responsibility and derives from his expertise.

Also incumbent on the worker is the task of building and nurturing the *relationship* that insures the best possible use of his service. Knowing oneself in the professional role involves understanding its demands on the giver . . . and the requirements for time and patience in building necessary trust. Of course, there is a range of extremes. The librarian performs her service within a few moments, and may require less time to build a fruitful relationship than, perhaps, the psychotherapist who may need many months. In each ease, however, the worker must reach out, set the "helping contract," and describe its context and content.

The *stance of the giver and the method of giving* are important. Giving a service indicates caring when it is offered with dignity. Conversely, offered without respect, it intensifies the independence-dependence struggle within the old person and often renders the service itself useless. Therefore, the manner in which service is offered is part of the offering itself.

The intergenerational component is also valuable. When the service-giver is a sensitive, helpful younger person, the social message of rejection is mitigated.

The service itself involves the dual considerations of context and content. A service offering is based on the idea that human health depends on the meeting of both physical and psychosocial needs. The latter includes the need for being cared about and loved, for opportunities to have, maintain, and express individual identity within a social context, for hope and a future, for maintaining a sense of self dignity through life's challenges. All services are related to these common human needs. Yet these fundamental tenets may be forgotten or ignored where an older person is concerned. How often do we see the service person (doctor, nurse, or social worker) communicating with a family member, "over the head," as it were, of the older person, who sits absently by as if these decisions were being made about someone else!

It is important that the worker believe in the values of his own service and in the integrity of his offer. The older person may have a stereotyped view of himself. He may have assumed that his condition is irreversible, or that his circumstances is inevitable, or that no change is possible, and that the service is futile. Just as such a view would limit the worker's offering of help so, too, will it limit the older person's willingness and capacity to use it.

It is important not only that the giver believe in his own service but also that it be given in such a way that the recipient believes in it also. One technique is active follow-up. For example, doctors in homes for the aged report that their patients often say, "What's the use. I'm an old woman. That's why I have these pains." Those doctors who are free of stereotypes and who believe in the efficacy of their medical offering respond that pain is not a necessary accompaniment of old age. But the response is not only verbal. They review the patient's condition as long as necessary, and they vary their treatment until the physical complaint is mitigated or treated in some way. *Both their stance and their service demonstrate their conviction that change and improvement are possible, and that the old person's stereotyped self-image is not valid.*

The worker who does not understand this may provide a less than adequate service. The doctor may prescribe palliatives instead of treatment. The recreationist may be satisfied with inappropriate and demeaning programs. "It's bingo time," says the activity leader, wheeling the protesting person to the game, not recognizing that in failing to respect and deal with the protests, she fails to accept the older person's individuality, and she violates his rights. The librarian may recommend a book inappropriately childish. The volunteer may shop for clothing unbecoming to the person, and so on, ad infinitum. Only by recognizing the integrity of the individual, and by respecting the value of his own service, can the helping person hope to provide an appropriate service.

Most of these ideas for dealing with older people are really applicable in giving help to people of all ages. This similarity, however, may be forgotten under the influence of a stereotype that denigrates the individual. Consequently, a service may be inappropriately or insensitively proffered.

A worker's expertise becomes the prop for one side of the service bridge. The other side involves the receiver. His strength and capacities must also be known. The provider of the service asks: Who is my recipient? What are his capacities at this moment in time? Which of these can be evoked to enable him to use my services most efficiently for himself? What motivation is required on my part?

The older person must be approached as a unique individual, recognized for the human being he is, respected for his past, and understood in terms of his life-style and coping capacities. His present needs must be clear to the worker. The service offering is based on his potential strengths, rather than on his possible (and, at the moment, exposed) weakness.

The helping agent appeals to a person's highest level of functioning. He imparts a realistic, but hopeful, view of such potential. For example, in the story "Be Friendly," the secretary who is the primary helper, takes the position that Mrs. Redmont can be helped to live at home rather than returning to the hospital. She makes her stance clear by the active support she offers both in the relationship and in the everyday, significant help she offers.

Enabling a person to utilize a service, thus exercising appropriate dependency, can free him to be more independent in other areas and can reveal to him his potential strengths. For example, the physiotherapist who helps a person learn to walk enables him to use the bathroom independently. Learning to utilize a shopping service (which for some people may require enormous adjustment) may be the crucial factor that enables a person to continue living in his own home.

Listening to a person's expression of his feelings and learning to decode his behavior are ways for a worker to assess strengths. Expressions of anger and hostility, for example, when a person is in a dependent and helpless situation may be a sign of his capacity and desire to work toward independence and control of his life. In "The Schoolteacher," Mrs. Herzog's anger and withdrawal were seen as expressions of her need to preserve her identity in the institution, and were accepted as signs of her strength.

Implicit in the service offering are the affirmations that:

1. The situation is not inevitable or irreversible. Change, treatment, amelioration, improvement, or cure are possible.

2. There are alternatives. A person need not be "locked in" to his problem.

3. It is not always the person who must "adjust" to a situation—sometimes situations must be adjusted to accommodate the individual. This view frees both the giver and the receiver to develop creative approaches and to seek alternatives.

4. The older person can have some control (no matter how limited, depending on circumstances) over his destiny. This view suggests that the older person should be involved in decision making and problem solving. Sometimes, involvement is mandated by the service. For example, no person can relearn walking without his being involved in the act of walking. Less obvious is his involvement in the decision making leading to the treatment. Sometimes, of course, such decision making is prescribed, for example, within so many weeks after a stroke a person must begin rehabilitation. But even this prescription assumes the motivation of the individual. When the motivation is lacking, as it may often be, passivity and resistance must be transformed into some level of active involvement if the help is to be effective. The service-giver, therefore, must appreciate the importance of motivation, and needs expertise in this area.

Sometimes it seems clear that the service cannot be given by the worker alone, or that someone else can provide it more readily. A visiting nurse may show a relative how to perform a nursing task. Sometimes, in an institution, the maintenance man can provide just the right word at the right time to encourage a person, or the nurse's aide will be the right person to help a patient practice a needed skill. In assessing these relationships and possibilities, the helping person is on the alert for all the strengths in the situation that will enable the older person to use needed help.

Sometimes, the problems are so knotty and complex that more than one discipline is needed. In this case, *a team* may collaborate. Each member of the team is then called on to make a decision concerning his particular expertise and how it may be integrated within a total helping plan. Again, this requires awareness of one's own offering, its relevance to the recipient, and its relationship to the other helping agents in the picture. Sometimes, the team relationships are very clear, for example, in an institution or hospital, roles are labeled and prescribed. Sometimes, the team is less obvious, since the "team member" may be a relative or a friend or someone else with whom the worker has little or no communication. In assessing resources, it is necessary to be aware of as many as possible, so that the receiver of help may be encouraged to use all that may be available. Sometimes, therefore, the strengths of the team are visible and at the worker's command. At other times, they are less visible, and are more likely at the command of the recipient. The helper must be aware, also, of the possible lack of strength. If a patient is too weak, the doctor will not prescribe walking. Similarly, the worker must know or learn what cannot be expected of a person or his situation and then must seek realistic alternatives.

In general, there are three broad categories of service. Each is interwoven with and affects the others. They represent different points of intervention in relation to people's needs, and different levels of preventive effort.

Maintenance and Supportive Services

These are usually offered during normal periods of life and are seen as alleviating stress, preventing crisis, and supporting independence by the appropriate meeting of dependency needs. Programs of public health, community psychiatry, social interaction, and community organization are services of this kind.

These services require a firm belief in their values. Prevention is quite undramatic and unspectacular. Hopefully, one will never see or experience that which is being prevented. It is hard to prove why something *did not happen*, since the success of this service lies in that very something never coming to pass! This can be frustrating to the service worker, who may feel unappreciated and unnoticed.

Yet, preventive services are very, very important. This type of service is one of the necessities in an improved world for everyone. They are the "built in" strengths to support strength. If the world were properly fashioned, if people's needs were adequately met, if preventive services were conceived and implemented, the community would need far less of the other types of services that are so expensive—financially, socially, and emotionally.

Another important note about preventive services is that they can be offered at many levels. That is, during times of health, prevention is a first line of service. But at any point of crisis, interventive service may be seen as preventing further crisis and breakdown.

Because the community is inadequately geared to prevention, this type of service is sometimes difficult to introduce both on the community level and to the individual. A person may feel he is "getting along all right" and may see a new service as a threat to his independence. Therefore, such services must be accompanied by community education so that they are perceived for their values and are not shunned for their threat. The presence of a service on the community scene extends an older person's horizons, and is a message to him that when he decides he needs or wants it, it will be available. The availability of preventive services, therefore, augment a person's capacity to control his life, and help support his independence. In "The Ashtray" a number of maintenance and supportive services and family activity enable Mr. Barker to remain living at home.

Crisis Interventive Services

Crisis, in its simplest terms, is defined as "an upset in a steady state."[2] Crisis carries a threat of qualitatively different proportions for older than for younger people. An older person may already be using all resources at his command to maintain some homeostasis in his life, and the crisis may upset it drastically by threatening a radical change.

Some common crises of the aged person involve illness and hospitalization. After recuperation, however, the older person may become less independent. Some basic changes in his life-style may become necessary as his capacity for self-care may be diminished and he may require more help. Illness and possible death of the spouse or caring person is another ever-present anxiety, as is the possibility of his own death.

Cath says, "perhaps the greatest stress on the adult human organism is in the last third of life."[3] A crisis situation exacerbates that stress. Offering service during a crisis period requires sensitivity, a sense of perspective and timing, and a recognition of the implications of the presenting crisis to the person's life and future.

In times of crisis, most people tend to behave differently from the way they do in less stressful times. The service person must be aware of the fear, tension, and anxiety that may be affecting the older person and his family. The danger of stereotyping is quite severe during such periods. The behavioral response to anxiety may be misinterpreted as mental illness or personality disorder. Also it is possible (for young or old) that the state of crisis may be accompanied by an acute mental disorder. In the circumstance of an older person's crisis, there is great danger that the stereotype of him will cause a misjudgment, ascribing an acute mental disorder to the aging process rather than to the actual situation. This can lead to improper diagnosis and treatment.

Rehabilitation Services

"Rehabilitate: To restore to a good condition."

The goal of a rehabilitation program is to restore a person to an improved state of physical health and vigor, to help him regain his emotional equilibrium, and to enable him, insofar as is possible, to return to family and community.

For the older person, these services are of great significance, since they may often spell the difference between extreme dependence and some measure of independence. It is most important, in this category of service, to expunge the rigidities of some of the stereotpyes of aging (for example, the irreversibility and inevitability of a dependent state) because rehabilitation efforts can be based only on the premise that some measure of improvement is possible.

Rehabilitation services are directed toward change. The very offering of such a service is a promise of hope and evokes the courage of the recipient. However, living things are endowed with the quality of inertia, or resistance to change. Furthermore, rehabilitation is offered in connection with unusual stress.

A person may be fearful that the effort will not yield results, or he may be too depressed or discouraged to try. He may, then, refuse service and may tax the patience of the service worker. Some old people, burdened by their self-image of dependency and their burning desire to remain independent, are unwilling to accept as their *right* the various forms of available assistance. Therefore, an outreach approach is vital, both in the individual offering and on the community level.

Sometimes a service is not used because other circumstances interfere. For example, a person might need help (transportation, a companion, and the like) to use the service. The totality of the recipient's circumstances must be considered when the plan is developed. Flexibility is needed. Sometimes the offer must be adapted to the recipient, instead of requiring the recipient to make all the accomodations.

Too often, the valuable effects of rehabilitation services may be thwarted by inadequacies at home or in the community. For example, an older person may regain some physical strength and may learn self-help skills while he is in an extended care facility, but the lack of necessary community facilities (housing or other supportive service) may make it impossible for him to return to the community. Similarly, there are often inadequate aftercare programs for a rehabilitated mental patient.

Some Community Needs

There is increasing recognition of the need for a variety of community programs to provide opportunities for continuity of care and supportive services that meet the needs of older people. Some services of this kind have been identified as follows:

Information and Counseling Services. Often people do not know where to seek assistance, what is available, or how to ask for it. A community information service identifies appropriate sources of help, makes referrals, can utilize flexible, creative outreach methods, and extends needed help in effective ways. Counseling enables a person to use this help appropriately.

Coordination Services. A person may lose the opportunity for service, or continuity of service, because the donors are not in communication with each other. Fragmentation of service, "hardening of the agency categories," poor interagency and interdisciplinary communication, all result in disservice to the needy older person and his family. The more needy the person, the more complex his problem, the greater the need for a coordinating agent.

Outreach Efforts. Service workers and their agencies must reach out to the individual (and family) and to the community to assure the use of services toward maximum possible independent functioning.

Auxiliary Services. (Transportation, shopping, volunteers, and friendly visiting) An integrated approach to need implies an altered system of service delivery based on a philosophy of "people-helping-people." This view is seen as beneficial to all sectors of community and population. Service workers are called on to broaden their views and their own roles within the service picture, to identify for themselves, and with each other, the potential offerings of each to the total well-being of the older person.

Diversification of Services and New Roles. Understanding new dimensions of need calls for a creative approach by all service professions, a new look at old role models, new ways of helping people, new sharing of tasks, even the development of new services and, perhaps, of new professions.

FOR EXAMPLE. Doctors and nurses are required to increase and utilize their knowledge and skills in the area of mental and social health, as well as physical health. Nurses are learning to work with patient (and family) groups in a variety of ways. Pharmacists work with other professionals in a range of settings involving the use of pharmaceuticals and medications. Lawyers are called on to understand and interpret the rights of older people, and to see that they are enforced. Teaching for service has become an act of involvement with practice as well as the sharing of knowledge and expertise. Social workers must expand their skills to include dealing with large and small groups of people and toward working in the community.

All professionals are required to improve their communication skills so that they can share their knowledge, teach skills, and provide consultation. They must learn to work together on teams with other professionals as well as with people less skilled than they are. This may include family members as well as paraprofessional and auxiliary workers. These are only *some* of the changes that are indicated for the definitions and functions of professional roles.

*   *   *

All these implications for service derive from a flexible, unstereotyped approach toward developing ways of meeting the range of needs of older people and their families.

Some Implications for Learning and Teaching

This "Album" offers the opportunity for students to "meet" the "story people" in the vignettes and to relate to them and to their experiences as fellow humans. This educational thrust suggests the value of explicating common factors in the human condition, enhancing the student's awareness of his own feelings and those of others, and connecting this awareness with the unique contributions of his discipline to the well-being of another person.

Points of emphasis in such a teaching program include: the identification of the student's own feelings about old people and their needs, as well as the nature and values of his services; the development of the sensitivity of the helping agent to the uniqueness of a given situation with regard to attitudes (as well as needs) of people being helped; and the understanding of the emotional components involved in giving and receiving help.

The teacher can encourage this learning by raising questions that highlight themes of common human concern. Students identify with situations illustrated in the vignettes through questions which ask them whether they have ever experienced similar circumstances; whether they have known others who have experienced similar circumstances; and, if so, to explore and describe the feelings and behavior associated with them.

Some of these questions that may be explored in different ways (for example, discussions, writings, and role plays) are:

1. How did the people in these vignettes anticipate and cope with some significant changes in their lives?

Some changes illustrated in the vignettes include:

Change in living arrangements: Aunt Becky, Coming Home, The Man, The Marriage, The Schoolteacher, Old Parents, Two Clients.

Role change: Coming Home, The Angry Giant, The Man, The Marriage, The Schoolteacher, Growing Old . . . Older . . . Old, Old Parents, My Advancing Years.

Changed relationships: Love, Loneliness, and Loss (poem), Letters of Two Men, The Ashtray, The Man, Be Friendly, The Schoolteacher, Old Parents.

Change in self-image or body image: The Angry Giant, The Schoolteacher, The Vegetable, The Man, The Ashtray, Be Friendly, Growing Old.

Change in life circumstances: All stories.

Changes in work role: Aunt Becky, The Ashtray, The Man, The Schoolteacher.

2. How did the "story people" deal with some of the problems of a "new beginning"; the need to sort out its traumas, to make new connections?

> *Examples:* The Marriage, The Haze Begins to Clear, Excerpts from Diary, The Schoolteacher, Old Parents, My Advancing Years.

3. Explore the impact of death (separation from a significant person, loss of a love object, or preparation for death) on some of the people in the stories.

> *Examples:* Aunt Becky, The Vegetable, Old People Talk of Death, Young People talk of Death, Letters of Two Men, Coming Home, Excerpts from a Diary, When I Think of Old People.

4. How did experience with traumatic or prolonged illness handicap or how did hospitalization affect the lives of the people in the vignettes?

> *Examples:* Aunt Becky, The Vegetable, Coming Home, The Haze Begins, to Clear, Be Friendly, The Schoolteacher, Two Clients, Old Parents.

5. Identify situations of reduced independence, increased dependency or the need for help.

All stories.

6. What are the issues and circumstances involved in the identity crises of some of the people in the stories? How did some of them try to affirm identity? What threats or insults to status or dignity were involved?

> *Examples:* Aunt Becky, Old Parents, Link to My Roots, The Vegetable, Two Clients, The Ashtray, The Schoolteacher, The Angry Giant,

The Man, Young People Discuss Aging, Getting Older . . .
Older . . . Old, How an 83-year-Old Man Looks at Life, Old
Parents, My Advancing Years, On Being Involved.

7. What were the threats to, or actual loss of control over self or circumstances in some of the vignettes?

Examples: Aunt Becky, The Vegetable, Love, Loneliness, and Loss
(poem), Letters of Two Men, Coming Home, The Ashtray, The
Angry Giant, The Man, The Schoolteacher, Young People Discuss Aging, Two Clients, Old Parents.

8. Which characters seem to have endured experiences with traumatic
or unreal qualities? With what other experiences may these be compared?

Examples: The Vegetable, Love, Loneliness, and Loss (poem), Coming
Home, The Ashtray, The Angry Giant, The Haze Begins to
Clear.

9. What are some of the situations that required the old people to cope
with feelings of fear or insecurity?

All stories.

10. How did these old people seek or use help from a stranger? What
feelings were involved, and how did the people cope with them?

Examples: Aunt Becky, The Vegetable, Love, Loneliness, and Loss
(poem), Be Friendly, Excerpts from a Diary, The Schoolteacher, Two Clients, A Sketch.

11. What efforts were attempted by some of the characters to compen-
sate for loss through relationship?

Examples: Young People Talk of Death, Letters of Two Men, The Ashtray, The Marriage, The Haze Begins to Clear, Be Friendly,
Experience with a Senior Citizen, Excerpts from a Diary, Getting Older . . . Older . . . Old, How an 83-Year-Old-Man looks at
Life, Old Parents, My Advancing Years, On Being Involved.

12. How did some of the central characters deal with feelings of guilt,
bitterness, or regret?

Examples: Coming Home, The Ashtray, The Angry Giant, The Schoolteacher, Two Clients.

13. What were the feelings of the younger people vis-a-vis the weakness,
dependency, or losses of the loved or formerly strong older person?

Examples: Coming Home, Letters of Two Men, Link to My Roots, Aunt
Becky, The Ashtray, The Man.

14. How did feelings of alienation and depression affect the survival activities of some of the characters? What kinds of help were extended and how
were they used or not used?

Examples: The Vegetable, Be Friendly, The Angry Giant, The Ashtray, A Sketch.

15. How did the people in the stories react to feelings of being unappreciated, deprecated, or rejected?

Examples: The Schoolteacher, The Man, The Angry Giant, Coming Home.

16. Under what circumstances did some people feel "out of place," and how did they handle it?

Examples: The Schoolteacher, Be Friendly, The Man, A Sketch.

17. In what ways did some of the characters want to be appreciated for their uniqueness, accepted for their commonalities?

Examples: Young Hearts with Old Faces, The Ashtray, The Vegetable, Young People Speak of Death, Young People Speak of Aging, The Schoolteacher, Be Friendly.

18. Evaluate the concerns and efforts of some of the "story people" in preparing for a new role; for example, a new task, a new position, a new lifestyle.

Examples: The Marriage, The Schoolteacher, Aunt Becky, Be Friendly, Young People Speak of Aging, Getting Older . . . Older . . . Old, How an 83 Year-old-Man Looks at Life, Old Parents, My Advancing Years, On Being Involved.

19. What are the messages in the stereotyping of some of the characters? What are the sources of such communication?

Examples: The Vegetable, Coming Home, The Ashtray, The Marriage, The Schoolteacher, Two Clients, Experience with a Senior Citizen, Young People Talk of Aging, When I Think of Old People, Getting Older . . . Older . . . Old, How an 83-Year-Old Man Looks at Life, Old Parents, My Advancing Years, On Being Involved.

20. What are the frustrations of the "story people" in enduring an experience that they were unable to interpret and for which there seemed to be no explanation?

Examples: The Angry Giant, When I Think of Old People, Love, Loneliness, and Loss (poem), The Man, The Vegetable, Two Clients.

21. How did some of the characters cope with the unexpected? What was involved in the response?

Examples: Aunt Becky, Experience with a Senior Citizen, Coming Home, The Ashtray, Getting Older . . . Older . . . Old, How an 83-Year-Old Man Looks at Life, Old Parents, My Advancing Years, On Being Involved.

22. How did some characters use "ego mechanisms of defense"? When were these functional? When dysfunctional?

Examples: Aunt Becky, Old Parents, The Schoolteacher, The Ashtray, The Angry Giant, Be Friendly, The Man, Two Clients, Getting Older . . . Older . . . Old, How an 83-Year-Old-Man Looks at Life, Old Parents, My Advancing Years, On Being Involved.

23. What is the significance of time in relation to the life circumstances of some of the characters? Too much time? Not enough time? Impatience?

Examples: Getting Older . . . Older . . . Old, How an 83-Year-Old Man Looks at Life, Old Parents, My Advancing Years, On Being Involved, The Angry Giant, Letters of Two Men, Love, Loneliness, and Loss (poem), The Marriage.

24. How did some "story people" search for sources of strength to cope with life circumstances?

Examples: Getting Older . . . Older . . . Old, How an 83-Year-Old Man Looks at Life, Old Parents, My Advancing Years, On Being Involved, The Ashtray, Letters of Two Men, The Haze Begins to Clear, The Schoolteacher, Be Friendly, Excerpts from a Diary, Old People Talk of Death.

25. What were the sources of life satisfaction for the central characters in these stories?

All stories.

26. How did the old people seek ways to be involved in experiences or relationships in spite of obstacles?

All stories.

27. What were some of the feelings of the helping person in the nonrewarding situation of some of the vignettes?

Examples: The Vegetable, Two Clients, Coming Home, The Angry Giant, Love, Loneliness, and Loss (poem).

These are some of the questions that offer themselves for exploration with students. The creative teacher will undoubtedly design many more.

The creative teacher will also devise ways of using the vignettes and related questions in keeping with an individual teaching style. These five methods may suggest others:

1. *Small group discussions.* The class is divided into small groups of no more than six people. Students are asked to share their own experiences related to a question or theme under discussion. After a suitable, brief period (15 to 20 minutes), the class reconvenes and shares its findings. In their discussion, student experiences are related to those described in the appropriate vig-

nettes. The teacher may explicate principles, may correlate and integrate differences and similarities, and may proceed to a number of other teaching points. A class experience of this kind provides a beginning point for identifying with some of the specific learning themes illustrated by the vignettes.

2. *Role Plays.* These may be introduced in varied ways (small groups, teacher-planned, or by being improvised in class) and may be designed to illustrate experiences connected with learning themes. Students may role play scenes from the vignettes or, better still, some of their own experiences. After a role play is presented, participants and observers are asked to comment on their feelings and thought associations. The teacher may then relate these appropriately to teaching points. Often, these role plays are so poignant and meaningful that very little explication is necessary.

3. *Tableaux or living sculpture.* A situation may be role played without words, using only the juxtaposition of figures to indicate relationships, or motion to illustrate interaction and struggle. Again, this technique enables the exploration of feelings and thought associations that often result in heightened insights and enhanced awareness.

4. *Writing assignments.* Creative writing (and its companion-method, literary readings) is useful in heightening awareness of feelings and demonstrates points of commonality among people. Through sharing their past experiences, and revealing their feelings, teachers and students risk exposure of their real selves and reach new levels of understanding. The revelations become springboards for improved relationships and fosters awareness of a shared fate despite an obvious diversity of backgrounds.

An assignment that often yields important learning asks the student to describe an experience or relationship with an older person. This may be assigned at the beginning of the program of learning about aging, and is useful in several ways.

(a) It helps a student focus on his own feelings and perceptions at this point in his learning.

(b) It identifies and highlights a relationship or experience that may be a starting point for new learning.

(c) It provides a point of comparison for the student later on in this learning experience.

Such descriptions of personal experiences should be included (with author's consent) in class bibliographies. Again, they offer the opportunity to identify with live experiences of peers and colleagues.

A second valuable writing assignment is to suggest that students keep a log of their thoughts and responses to the total learning experiences of the semester, for example, class, fieldwork (if any), personal experiences, reactions to readings, discussions, and the like. Such a writing assignment helps a student think through these various components of the educational experience —and to integrate them in a uniquely individual and meaningful way.

5. *Encounter.* Students may be asked to meet and interact with (at least) one older person, to describe this encounter and its meaning to him. For both assignments, (nos. 4 and 5) the vignettes may provide a backdrop and point of comparison for the student's own experience. Related themes, identified in the questions, offer a basis for analyzing the experience. Encounters may be in dyads, or in groups. Intergenerational "rapp sessions" in which young and old share their ideas are exciting learning experiences for all. These may be held in the classroom by inviting some older people to join the class, or elsewhere—by taking the class on a field trip at the invitation of a group of elders.

6. *A joint project.* Involving the class in a shared experience with older people is another educational media. The class members might wish to provide a service (for example, present a play or concert), or share a service (for example, volunteer together with some elderly community volunteers), or share a learning experience such as an art class, a current events discussion, or a social action or planning session. In any case, the experience itself will yield to interpretation through log, story, discussion, or further explication of learning and change.

. . .

This book has been shaped, in part, by the student responses to assignments, some of which are offered here as examples. When "Two Clients" was included in the class bibliography, one student wrote:

"I like the personal pieces . . . especially the one by N. B. Because it was personal, it was full of emotion that touched me. I had a sense of the pervading brutality of our institutions and our system after reading N. B.'s description of Mrs. S's death. And yet, I also had feelings of hope. An individual *can* bridge the system and touch people. . . ."

Another student wrote in her log about the effects of the readings, role plays, and discussion on her "stereotyped thinking." She said:

"In reading 'An Experience with Older People' and 'Mental Illness in Aging,' I became more alert to the problems of the aged. . . . I have been guilty of stereotyping the aged—which takes their problems and the myths and makes their position more vulnerable and undesirable . . . . 'Helping' the aged is the same process as helping others. . . . The major problem here is the lack of knowledge and the abundance of myth about the aged that makes these social work tasks so much harder. . . . It's hard for me to believe that the only close older person I've known defies the stereotype, and yet I fell into the habit of accepting and fearing it. My own grandmother is 76, wise, intelligent and full of life. . . . Yet, I told my advisor, when we discussed a placement last fall, that I did not want to work with the aged. When she talked about stereotypes and consequent fears of working with these people, I recognized my own illusions. At least I could see myself. But it is only now—10 months later—that I can begin to say I'm growing out of this."

Finally, another thoughtful student summed up his views in a long paragraph that, in effect, reflects the educational thrust of this album. He wrote

"This book, designed for teaching, indicates some specific ways of thinking about older adults. Your ideas are based on a positive outlook of life, people and the aging process. The problem lies in the difference between your mode of thought and the general climate of opinion. Although individuals may have positive thoughts about elderly people close to them (e.g. their grandparents), they have been socialized to think about older adults as a group in a negativistic and stereotpyed way. This book requires the reader to change such thought patterns and try to accept the positive approach which may be diametrically opposite from his present outlook."

In essence, this statement encapsulates this album's challenge to both student and teacher.

Notes on the Vignettes

Life, Work and Death

Aunt Becky

This is a straightforward, unfictionalized account of a case known to a number of social agencies. All incidents actually occurred. Only the names have been changed. Many of the reader-judges felt that Aunt Becky had so many problems, she must have been a composite. In fact, incredible as it may seem, this woman had several additional problems in her family life with which she was coping. She is no composite!

The Vegetable

Mrs. Talbott was a patient in a nursing home. The case history presented through her thoughts, is based on the real material insofar as it is known to the staff. The outreach efforts of the worker here, represent those of several disciplines, for example, the nurse, occupational therapist, social worker, and others who tried to reach the patient. The patient's thoughts, as projected here, are, of course, the speculation of the author.

Old People Talk About Death

These are excerpts of a taped discussion held with a mental health group of aged women-residents in a nursing home. The group is led by a psychotherapist and is part of a program aimed at developing and maintaining a therapeutic atmosphere in the home. This piece evoked controversial comments from the reader-judges. Some were critical, while others were complimentary, about the techniques of the therapist; some felt the subject was morbid and painful; others discussed their own feelings about death. These differences of opinion suggest that this piece offers much learning for the thoughtful reader.

Young People Talk About Death

This is excerpted from taped discussions with a group of teenage campers in a work program of a summer camp. Their assignment was to participate in an activity-and-social-service program at a nearby nursing home. This discussion was part of a supervisory seminar led by the author.

So Live!

This is a true story of an elderly woman discharged from the hospital and referred for supportive services to a community agency. The thoughts of the woman were shared with her worker. Only the name is changed.

Love, Loneliness, and Loss

The Marriage

The two people in this story were married, as described, and returned to live in the same home for aged people about three years later. The story was reported in the local newspaper. Some reader-judges felt this was "saccharine"; others questioned whether the administrator could really have been so understanding; while still others questioned the attitudes of the offspring. These are all telling responses related to the stereotypes this *Album* seeks to dispell.

Coming Home

This story was written by a college student. She is describing her own experience, and her feelings about her family situation.

The Ashtray

Mr. Barker is a member of a senior citizens program in a community center. He was known to the author. Home visits were made by a social worker who also worked with the family. The incidents and situations are real. The conversations are fictionalized.

Letters of Two Men

These are authentic letters written by two elderly men in their late seventies. They are unedited and unfictionalized. The names have been changed. Reader-judges questioned their authenticity because of the sentimental, florid literary style. Others questioned "the depth of feeling in an old man such a long time after his wife died." Still others commented that "such feelings do not pertain only to old age." Such comments suggest fruitful thoughts and discussion by readers.

The Angry Giant

This man was a resident in a home for aged blind people. In an effort to help him express his emotions, lift his depression somewhat, help him clear some of his anger and begin to cope with his blindness and institutionalization —he was encouraged to dictate his memoirs to the author. The incidents described in the poem were recalled by him during these sessions. The emotions expressed here were shared by him with the author.

Neighbors

These two couples, black and white, were personally known to the author. The story occurred as described. The identities are changed.

Old People Talk About Sex

Social attitudes (community, family, staff, and old people, themselves) plus institutional architecture and atmosphere combine to make sex a taboo and difficult subject for discussion. What does this free-flowing discussion suggest about the real needs of people, and about the atmosphere and relationships in a group therapy program?

Change, Hope, and Struggle

The Haze Begins to Clear

The poem is based on the remarks by a member of an admissions group in a home for the aged blind. This group was developed to help the newly admitted residents with their difficulties in coping with their new problems of communal living.

Be Friendly

This is a true account of a resident in an apartment house for elderly people. Mrs. Redmont had just returned from a mental hospital. All the events actually occurred. The mail incident, the medication, the feelings and actions of the tenants are all part of the case study. Mary, the secretary, is a composite of two secretaries who undertook the tasks described here and who worked with the consultation of a social worker. Reader-judges asked "where do you find such secretaries?" Some questioned whether these incidents actually occurred. Others said, "If it isn't real, it should be."

The Schoolteacher

This schoolteacher was a resident at a home for aged blind people for eight years. Every incident, including the "about-face" in her attitude toward Mrs. Rose, another resident, is unfictionalized. The Home published two books of verses written by her during her residence. The verses are quoted from case material.

Excerpts from the Diary of a Social Worker

These are verbatim excerpts from actual case records of a social work student. They have been edited for diction and grammar only.

The Man

This story is based on case material about a family that came to the author for consultation. The actual incident, but not its contents, is fictionalized. Since this story was written, "Carlo" died. He was never to leave his beloved home.

A Sketch

This incident occurred as recounted. Only the names have been changed.

An Open Letter to a Young Doctor

This letter was actually written to an attending physician in a hospital, after the author had visited the elderly patient. The incident that occasioned this note occurred as described. Many professionals, and other helping agents, are unaware of their stereotyped attitudes toward old people. What questions are raised concerning services, families, and feelings?

Young People Write of Aging

Young Hearts with Old Faces and When I Think of Old People

These were written by students in their senior year of high school in response to a session on aging led by the author.

Young People Discuss Aging

These excerpts are from a verbatim taped session of the same group of teenage campers who participated in the discussion in Young People Talk About Death. The discussion was led by the author.

Two Clients

This vignette was written by a student in a graduate school of social work. This is a straightforward, unfictionalized account of his experiences as a caseworker in the New York City Department of Social Services.

Link to My Roots and Experience with a Senior Citizen

Both of these vignettes were written by students at a graduate school of social work. They were submitted in fulfillment of written assignments at the beginning of their year of fieldwork placement with older adults.

Old People Write of Aging

Getting Old . . . Old . . . Older

This was written by a 77-Year-old housewife who is an active wife, mother, grandmother, and worker in the community in which she lives.

How an 83-Year-Old Man Looks at Life

The author is a retired professional who is still involved with both professional and social organizations. He continues to read and write extensively for his own pleasure, for his family, and friends.

My Advancing Years and On Being Involved

Both of these vignettes were written by women in their early seventies. These women are active in a Geriatric Housing Committee, a social action program in their community.

Old Parents

This poem was written in Yiddish by a resident in a home for aged blind people. She was a participant in the group life at this home and wrote for its newspaper and literary publications. This poem was written shortly after she began her residence at the home, and was part of her own effort to accept the difficulties of institutional living and their challenge to her. The poem was translated by the author of the *Album*.

Footnotes and References

Footnotes refer to editions or individual works cited in the Bibliography.

Viewing Aging and Learning in Our Times

1. Herman B. Brotman, *Who are the Aged: A Demographic View*, pp. 1–9.
2. Group for the Advancement of Psychiatry, Committee on Aging, *Toward a Public Policy on Mental Health Care of the Elderly*, 664.
3. Ibid, p. 672.
4. John W. Gardner, *Self-Renewal*, p. xiii.
5. Nevitt Sanford, "Human Problems Institute and General Education" in *Creativity and Learning*, edited by Jerome Kagan, p. 207.
6. Susanne K. Langer, *Problems of Art*, p. 15.
7. Maxine Green, "The Humanities and Social Work Education," *Journal of Education for Social Work, II* (1966), 21–31.

8. Irving Rosow, "Old Age: One Moral Dilemma of an Affluent Society," *The Gerontologist, II* (1962), 191.

The Challenge

1. Marjorie B. Tiven *Older Americans*, p. vii.
2. Herman B. Brotman, "A Profile of the Older American," p. 223.
3. Brotman, *Who are the Aged*, p. 3.
4. Ibid, p. 5.
5. Herman B. Brotman, *Facts and Figures on Older Americans*, p. 2.
6. Louis Lowy, "Meeting the Needs of Older People on a Differential Basis," *Social Group Work with Older People* p. 45.
7. Brotman, *Who Are the Aged*, p. 10.
8. Brotman, "Profile of the Older American," pp. 222–223.

The World of the Aging Person

1. Brotman, *Facts and Figures*, p. 1.
2. Tiven, *Older Americans*, p. 1.
3. National Council on Aging, *The Golden Years*, p. 1.
4. Brotman, "Profile of the Older American." He also reports that, "The national median income of families with heads aged over 65 is $5,053, and of individual aged, $1,951. Only 10 percent have more than $10,000 annual income," p. 221.
5. Tiven, op. cit., p. 8.
6. Brotman, *Facts and Figures*, p. 10.
7. Lowy, "Meeting Needs of Older People," pp. 24 and 47.
8. NCOA, *The Golden Years*, p. 1.
9. Matilda White Riley, *Aging and Society, I*, 165.
10. Helen Z. Lopata, "The Social Involvement of American Widows," *American Behavioral Scientist, XIV*, (September–October 1970) 41057.
11. Ibid, p. 56.
12. Riley, op. cit., pp. 167–170.
13. Margaret Blenkner, "Normal Dependencies of Aging," *The Dependencies of Old People*, edited by Richard A. Kalish, p. 29.
14. Tiven, op. cit. p. 14.
15. M. Powell Lawton and Morton H. Kleban, "The Aged Resident of the 'Inner City,' " *The Gerontologist, XI* (1971), 280.
16. NCOA, *Golden Years*, p. 4.
17. Rachel Cowan, "The New Minority: Senior Citizens and Victims of Gerontocide," *The Village Voice*, January 21, 1971, p. 5.

18. NCOA, op. cit., p. 23.

19. Tiven, op. cit. p. 16.

20. Richard A. Kalish, ed., *Dependencies of Old People*, p. 6.

21. Blenker, op. cit. p. 27.

22. NCOA, *Golden Years*, p. 139.

Myths and Stereotypes

1. Tiven, *Older Americans*, p. 34.

2. Robert N. Butler, "Myths and Realities of Aging".

3. Riley, *Aging and Society, II,* 7.

4. Jerome Kaplan, "Practitioners: Their Functions and Settings, Training Needs and New Potentials," *Working with Older People, A Guide to Practice, III,* 11.

5. Bernard Strehler, "Ten Myths About Aging," p. 9.

6. Ethel Shanas, "The Aged Report on Their Health Problems," *Aging in Modern Society,* edited by Simon and Epstein, p. 61.

7. Lester Breslow, "The Public Health Problem," *Aging in Modern Society,* p. 53.

8. Muriel Oberleder, "Psychological Characteristics," pp. 1–3.

9. John Arsenian, "Situational Factors," pp. 667 and 674.

10. Butler, "Myths and Realities of Aging," p. 35.

11. U. S. Department of Health, Education, and Welfare, *Biological, Psychological and Sociological Aspects of Aging,* Vol. II, *Working with Older People: A guide to Practice,* p. 35.

12. Group for Advancement of Psychiatry, *Psychiatry and the Aged, V,* 567.

13. U. S. Department of Health, Education, and Welfare, *Practitioner and the Elderly,* Vol. I, *Working with Older People,* August 1966, p. 39.

14. Oberleder, "Psychological Characteristics," p. 16.

15. Brotman, "Profile of the Older American," p. 3.

16. Brotman, *Who are the Aged,* p. 5.

17. Ewald E. Busse, "Social Forces Influencing the Care and Health of the Elderly," *Aging and Social Policy,* edited by McKinney and De Vyver.

18. Tiven, op. cit. p. 40.

19. Elaine M. Brody, "Social Work Practice," p. 5.

20. Blenkner, "Normal Dependencies of Aging," p. 32.

21. Ethel Shanas, ed., "Older People and Their Families," *The Multigeneration Family: Papers on Theory and Practice* (Trenton, N. J.: Department of State, Division on Aging, 1964), p. iii.

Tasks of the Individual

1. Eric Erickson, *Identity and the Life Cycle*.
2. Ruth Benedict, "Continuities and Discontinuities in Cultural Conditioning," *Social Perspectives on Behavior*, edited by Stein and Cloward, p. 172.
3. Herman Stein and Richard Cloward, "Introduction to Social Roles," *Social Perspective on Behavior*, p. 172.
4. Tiven, *Older Americans*, p. 19.
5. Alfred H. Lawton, "Characteristics of the Geriatric Person," *The Gerontologist, VIII* (Summer 1968), 120–23.
6. Charlotte Buhler, "Theoretical Observations About Life's Basic Tendencies," *Journal of Psychotherapy, XIII* (1959), 561–581.
7. Charlotte Buhler, "Meaningful Living in the Mature Years," in R. W. Kleemeier, *Aging and Leisure*, p. 368.
8. Clarke and Anderson, *Culture and Aging*, pp. 398 ff.
9. R. Peck, "Psychological Developments in the Second Half of Life," *Psychological Aspects of Aging*, edited by J. E. Anderson, pp. 42–53.

Background Discussions

1. Stanley H. Cath, "Some Dynamics of the Middle and Later Years," *Crisis Intervention: Selected Readings*, edited by Howard J. Parad p. 175.
2. This definition was developed by Gerald Caplan in seminars at the Harvard School of Public Health, 1959 to 1960, as reported by Lydia Rappaport, "The State of Crisis." *Crisis Intervention* edited by Parad, p. 24.
3. Cath, op. cit. p. *174ff*.

Bibliography

"The Aged in America." *American Red Cross Youth Journal, XLVII* (February, 1971), 3.

Allport, Gordon, *Letters from Jenny*. New York: Harcourt, Brace & World, 1965.

Anderson, J. E., ed. *Psychological Aspects of Aging*. Washington, D.C.: American Psychological Association, 1956.

Arsenian, John. "Situational Factors Contributing to Mental Illness in Elderly." *Geriatrics*, October, 1962, pp. 667–74.

Arth, M. J. "An Interdisciplinary View of the Aged." *Journal of Geriatric Psychiatry*, 1968, pp. 33–39.

Ashley, Montague Francis. *On Being Human*. New York: H. Shuman, 1950.

Baer, P. E.; Morin, K.; and Gaitz, C. M. "Familial Resources of Elderly Psychiatric Patients." *Archives of General Psychiatry, XXII* (1970), 343–50.

Barnett, Abraham Nathaniel. "Beyond Librarianship: A Critique of Rationales of Special Library Service to the Aged." *Library Quarterly, XXXI* (April, 1961), 178–86.

Becker, Arthur, H., and Weisman, Avery D. "The Patient with a Fatal Illness —To Tell or Not to Tell." *Journal of the American Medical Association*, CCI (August, 1967), 646–48.

"Being Old in the Country of the Young." *Vista Volunteer, VI* (August, 1970).

Beinzel, Joseph H. "Gerentophobia—Some Remarks on a Social Policy for the Elderly." *The Humanist*, July/August, 1970, pp. 17–18.

Bendkowski, B. "Incapacitating Diseases in the Elderly: A Survey in General Practice." *Journal of the American Geriatrics Society, XVI* (1968), 1340–45.

Beresford, John C., ed. *Living in the Multigenerational Family*. Ann Arbor, Mich.: Michigan State University, 1969.

Berezin, Martin A., and Cath, Stanley H. *Geriatric Psychiatry*. New York: International Universities Press, 1965.

Berzon, Fay Clark. "Use of Extended Care Facility for Beginning Students." *Nursing Outlook, VIII* (November 1970), 44–46.

Bieber, Margaret. "Letter on Her 90th Birthday." *Columbia Forum, XIII* (Fall 1970), 37.

Birren, James E., ed. *Handbook of Aging and the Individual: Psychological and Biological Aspects.* Chicago: Chicago University Press, 1960.

Block, Barbara. "Reflections on a Process I Don't Want to Be Part Of." *The Junior League Magazine,* July/August, 1970, pp. 13–17.

Blumenthal, H. T. *Medical and Clinical Aspects of Aging.* New York: Columbia University Press, 1962.

Bogomolitz, V. *The Secret of Keeping Young:* London: Arco Press, 1954.

Bourne, G. H. *Structural Aspects of Aging.* New York: Hafner, 1945.

Bredemeir, Harry C., and Toby, Jackson. *Social Problems in America.* New York: Wiley, 1960.

Brim, Orville G., Jr., and others. *The Dying Patient.* New York: Russell Sage Foundation, 1970.

Brockington, Fraser, and Lempert, Susanne M. *Social Needs of Over-80's, The Stockport Survey.* Manchester: Manchester University Press, 1966.

Brody, Elaine M. "Serving the Aged: Educational Needs as Viewed by Practice." *Social Work, XV* (October 1970), 42–51.

———. "Social Work Practice with the Aged." *Abstracts for Social Workers.* New York. National Association of Social Work, 1971.

———, and Silverman, H. "Individualized Treatment of the Mentally Impaired Aged." *Social Work Practice.* New York: Columbia University Press, 1970.

Brotman, Herman B. "Every Tenth American." *Adding Life to Years.* Iowa: University of Iowa, October, 1968.

———. *Facts and Figures on Older Americans.* Washington, D.C.: U.S. Government Printing Office, 1971.

———. "A Profile of the Older American." *Long Range Programs and Needs in Aging and Related Fields,* Washington, D.C.: U.S. Government Printing Office, 1968.

———. *Who Are the Aged: A Demographic View.* Ann Arbor, Mich.: University of Michigan, 1968.

Brown, Lucille Esther. *Patients Are People. New Dimension of Patient Care.* Vol. III. New York: Russell Sage Foundation, 1963.

Brown, Myrtle Irene. *Nurses Attitudes Toward the Aged and Their Care.* Washington, D.C.: United States Public Health Service, 1967.

Brown, O. Taylor. "The Teaching of Clinical Geriatrics to Undergraduate Medical Students." *The Gerontologist, XI* (Autumn 1971), 250–53.

Bruhn, John G. "An Ecological Perspective of Aging." *The Gerontologist, II* (Winter 1971), 318–21.

Buhler, Charlotte. "Theoretical Observations About Life's Basic Tendencies." *Journal of Psychotherapy, XIII* (1959), 561–81.

Burgess, E. W., ed. *Aging in Western Societies.* Chicago: University of Chicago Press, 1960.

Butler, Robert N. "Myths and Realities of Aging." Address at Governor's Conference on Aging, Columbia, Md., May 28, 1970. (Mimeographed.)

————. "Why Are Older Consumers So Susceptible?" *Geriatrics, XXIII* (1968), 83–88.

Campbell, Margaret C. "Study of the Attitudes of Nursing Personnel Toward the Geriatric Patient." *Nursing Research, XX* (March-April 1971), 147–51.

Carp, F. M. "Differences Among Older Workers, Volunteers, and Persons Who Are Neither." *Journal of Gerontology, XXIII* (1968), 497–507.

Carpenter, D. G., and Loynd, J. A. "An Integrated Theory of Aging." *Journal of the American Geriatrics Society, XVI* (1968), 1307–22.

Cassirer, Ernst. *Language and Myth.* New York: Harper and Brothers, 1946.

Clark, E. "Improving Post-Hospital Care for Chronically Ill Elderly Patients." *Social Work, XIV* (1969), 62–67.

Clark, Margaret. "Patterns of Aging Among the Elderly Poor of the Inner City." *The Gerontologist, XI* (Spring 1971), 58–66.

————, and Anderson, Barbara Gallatin. *Culture and Aging.* Springfield, Ill.: Charles C. Thomas, 1967.

Coe, Rodney, M. "Professional 'Stereotypes' Hamper Treatment of Aged." *Geriatric Focus, XV* (September 15, 1966), 1–3.

————, Zibit, Samuel, and Perrin, Margaret. "Introduction to Interdisciplinary Perspectives on Aging." *The Gerontologist, VIII* (Spring 1968), 1–3.

Cohen, Ruth G. "Graduate School Work Training in a Multipurpose Geriatric Center." *The Gerontologist, XI* (1971), 352–56.

Comfort, A. *Aging: The Biography of Senescence.* New York: Holt, Rinehart, and Winston, 1964.

————. "Biological Theories of Aging." *Human Development, XIII* (1970), 127–39.

"Commune for the Elderly Challenged." *The New York Times,* August 7, 1971, p. 26.

Community Service Society. *The Elderly and the State Mental Hospitals.* New York: The Society, 1969.

Conti, Mary Louise. "The Loneliness of Old Age." *Nursing Outlook, XVIII* (August 1970), 85.

Coser, L. A. *Sociology Through Literature.* New York: Prentice Hall, 1963.

Council on Social Work Education. "Fay Carson." *Teaching Record,* No. 159. New York: The Council, 1964.

————. *Homemaker-Home Health Aide Service to the Aged and Chronically Ill.* New York: The Council, 1968.

————. *A Literary Bibliography on Aging.* New York: The Council, 1968.

————. *Night Fears and Loneliness, Working with the Terminally Ill and Aged.* New York: The Council, 1968.

————. *Teachers Source Book on Aging.* New York: The Council, 1964.

Cowan, Rachel. "The New Minority: Senior Citizens and Victims of Gerontocide." *The Village Voice,* January 21, 1971.

Cumming, Elaine. "New Thoughts on the Theory of Disengagement." *International Journal of Psychiatry, VI* (1968) 53–67.

———, and Henry, William E. *Growing Old.* New York: Basic Books, 1961.

De Beauvoir, Simone. *Old Age.* New York: G. P. Putnam, 1972.

Deropp, R. S. *Man Against Aging.* New York: St. Martin's Press, 1960.

Elfenbaum, Arthur. "Refusal of Dentists to Recognize and Adjust to Physiologic Changes in Aged. 'A Major Problem.' " *Geriatric Focus, VI* (March 15, 1967), 1.

Englebardt, Stanley L. "Your Mother Died Three Years Ago." *Today's Health, XLIX* (March 1971), 65–68.

Erikson, Eric. *Identity and the Life Cycle.* New York: International Universities Press, 1959.

Esposito, S. J.; Vinton, P. W.; and Rapuano, J. A. "Nutrition in the Aged; A Review of the Literature." *Journal of American Geriatrics Society, XVII* (1969), 790–806.

Feifel, Henry, ed. *The Meaning of Death.* New York: McGraw Hill, 1959.

Field, Minna. *Aging with Honor and Dignity.* Springfield, Ill.: Charles C. Thomas, 1968.

Frankel, F. H., and Clark, E. "Mental Health Consultation and Education in Nursing Homes." *Journal of the American Geriatrics Society, XVII* (1969), 360–65.

Freeman, J. T. *Clinical Features of the Older Patient.* Springfield, Ill.: Thomas, 1965.

———. "A Survey of Geriatric Education: Catalogues of United States Medical Schools." *Journal of American Geriatric Society, XIX* (September 1971), 746–63.

Freud, Sigmund. *Mourning and Melancholia.* London: Hogarth Press, 1957.

Fulsom, Robert. *Use of Reality Therapy Technique in Treatment of Mental Illness.* Tuscaloosa, Ala.: Veterans Administration Hospital, 1970.

Gage, Frances Boland. "Suicide in the Aged." *American Journal of Nursing, LXXI (November* 1971), 21–53.

Gaitz, Charles M. "The Coordinator: An Essential Member of a Multidisciplinary Team Delivering Health Services to Aged Persons." *The Gerontologist, X* (1970), 217–20.

———, and others. *Goals of Comprehensive Health Care in Advanced Old Age.* Ann Arbor, Mich.: University of Michigan, 1968.

Gardner, John. "Remarks at Opening Session of 14th Annual Program of Council on Social Workers Education." *Journal of Education for Social Work, II* (Spring 1966), 5–9.

———. *Self-Renewal.* New York: Harper and Row, 1964.

Geriatric Focus. Orange, N. J.: Knoll Pharmaceutical Company, September 1961-December 1970.

Gordon, Susan, and Vinacke, W. E. "Self- and Ideal Self-Concepts and Dependency of Aged Persons Residing in Institutions." *Journal of Gerontology, XXVI* (July 1971), 337–43.

Gossett, Helen. "Restoring Identity to Depersonalized Residents in Nursing Homes." New York: United Hospital Fund, 1966. (Mimeographed.)

Greene, Maxine. "The Humanities and Social Work Education." *Journal of Education for Social Work, II* (1966), 21–31.

Group for Advancement of Psychiatry. *The Aged and Community Mental Health, A Guide to Program Development.* New York: GAP, 1971.

————. *Education for Community Psychiatry.* New York: GAP, 1967.

————. *Psychiatry and the Aged.* New York: GAP, 1965.

————, Committee on Aging. *Toward a Public Policy on Mental Health Care of the Elderly.* New York: GAP, 1970.

Hall, Lydia. "A Center for Nursing." *Nursing Outlook,* 1963.

Hanford, J. "New Pressures on Family Life." *Social Casework, L* (1969), 3–9.

Haun, Paul. *Recreation: a Medical Viewpoint.* New York: Bureau of Publication, Teachers College, Columbia University, 1965.

Henry, Jules. *Culture Against Man.* New York: Random House, 1965.

Henry, William. "The Theory of Intrinsic Disengagement." Paper presented at the International Gerontological Research Seminar, Markaryd, Sweden, 1963. (Mimeographed.)

Hersey, Jean, and Hersey, Robert. *These Rich Years—A Journal of Retirement.* New York: Scribner's, 1969.

Hickey, Tom; Hickey, Louise A.; and Kalish, Richard A. "Children's Perceptions of the Elderly." *Journal of Genetic Psychology, XXIII* (1968), 227–35.

Hickey, T., and Kalish, R. "Young People's Perceptions of Adults." *Journal of Gerontology, XXIII* (1968), 215–19.

Hoffman, Adeline M., ed. *The Daily Needs and Interests of Older People.* Springfield, Ill.: Charles C. Thomas, 1970.

Howell, Sandra C. "Applied Research Needs in Nutrition and Aging." *The Gerontologist,* Spring 1970, p. 73.

————, and Loeb, Martin B. ed., *Nutrition and Aging.* Washington, D.C. Gerontological Society, Fall 1969.

Howell, Trenor H. *A Student's Guide to Geriatrics.* 2nd ed. Springfield, Ill.: Charles C. Thomas, 1970.

"I grow old . . . I grow old." *Johns Hopkins Magazine,* Spring 1968.

Jackson, N. "The Occupational Therapist As Consultant to the Aged." *American Journal of Occupational Therapy, XXIV* (November/December 1970), 572–75.

Jacobs, Lee H. *Youth Looks at Aging: An Approach to Content for a Unit of Study on the Aging at the Secondary School Level: A Teacher's Guide for a Unit of Three or Four Weeks.* 2nd ed. Iowa City: University of Iowa, 1969.

————, and others. *Education for Aging: A Review of Recent Literature.* Syracuse, N.Y.: ERIC Clearing House on Adult Education, 1970.

Kagan, Jerome, ed. *Creativity and Learning.* Boston: Beacon Press, 1970.

Kahana, B., and Kahana, E. "Changes in Mental Status of Elderly Patients in Age-Related and Age-Segregated Hospital Milieus." *Journal of Abnormal Psychology, LXXV* (1970), 177–81.

Kalish, Richard A., ed. *The Dependencies of Old People.* Ann Arbor, Mich.: University of Michigan, 1969.

————, and Yuen, Sam. "Americans of East Asian Ancestry: Aging and The Aged." *The Gerontologist, II* (Spring 1971), 36–48.

Kaplan, Oscar J., ed. *Mental Disorders in Later Life.* Stanford, Calif.: Stanford University Press, 1956.

Kastenbaum, Robert. "Multiple Perspectives on a Geriatric 'Death Valley.' " *Community Mental Health Journal, III* (Spring 1967), 21–29.

————, ed. *New Thoughts on Old Age.* New York: Springer Publishing Company, 1964.

Kaufman, Ralph M. *The Psychiatric Unit in a General Hospital—Its Current and Future Role.* New York: International Universities Press, 1965.

Kazzaz, D. S., and Vickers, R. "Geriatric Staff Attitudes Toward Death." *Journal of the American Geriatrics Society, XVI* (1968), 1364–74.

Kent, Donald P. "The Elderly in Minority Groups; Variant Patterns of Aging." *The Gerontologist, XI* (Spring 1971), 26–29.

————. "The Negro Aged." *The Gerontologist, II* (Spring, 1971), 48–52.

Kiefer, Christie W. "Notes on Anthropology and the Minority Elderly." *The Gerontologist, XI* (Spring 1971), 94–98.

Kiell, N. *The Adolescent Through Fiction.* New York: International Universities Press, 1959.

Kleemeire, Robert W. *Aging and Leisure.* New York: Oxford University Press, 1961.

Knox, J. W., and Paterson, J. E. "Assessing the Social Circumstances of the Elderly by Screening." *Medical Social Work, XXI* (1969) 235–41.

Kogan, Nathan, and Wallach, Michael. "Age Changes in Values and Attitudes." *Journal of Gerontology, XVI* (1961), 272–80.

Koller, Marvin R. *Social Gerontology.* New York: Random House, 1968.

Korenchevsky, V., and Bourne, J. H., eds. *Physiological and Pathological Aging.* New York: Hafner, 1961.

Korson, S. M. "From Custodial Care to Intensive Treatment of the Geriatric Patient." *Journal of the American Geriatrics Society, XVI* (1968), 1107–13.

Kubler-Rose, Elizabeth. *On Death and Dying.* New York: Macmillan, 1969.

Kushner, R. E., and Bunch, M. E., eds. *Graduate Education in Aging Within the Social Sciences.* Ann Arbor, Mich.: University of Michigan, 1967.

Kutner, Bernard, and others. *500 Over Sixty*. New York: Russell Sage Foundation, 1956.

Lamont, Corliss. *A Humanist Funeral Service*. San Francisco: American Humanist Association, 1970.

Langer, Susanne K. *Feeling and Form*. New York: Scribner's Sons, 1953.

————. *Problems of Art*. New York: Scribner's, 1957.

Lawton, Alfred J. "Characteristics of the Geriatric Person." *The Gerontologist, VIII* (Summer 1968), 120–23.

Lawton, M. Powell. "The Functional Assessment of Elderly People." *Journal of the American Geriatrics Society, XIX* (June 1971), 465–81.

————, and Morton, H. Kleban. "The Aged Resident of the 'Inner City.' " *The Gerontologist, XI* (1971), 277–83.

————, and Yaffe, Silvia. "Mortality, Morbidity, and Voluntary Change of Residence by Older People." *Journal of American Geriatric Society, XVIII* (October 1970), 823–31.

Leichter, Hope Jense, and Mitchell, William E. *Kinship and Casework*. New York: Russell Sage Foundation, 1967.

Leonard, George B. *Education and Ecstasy*. New York: Dell, 1968.

Lewis, Charles N. "Reminiscing and Self Concept in Old Age." *Journal of Gerontology, XXVI* (April 1971), 240–43.

Lindley, Donald. "Therapeutic Recreation—An Approach." Supplement to *Adding Life to Years*. Iowa City, Ia.: University of Iowa, July 1970.

Lipman, A., and Sterne, R. S. "Ascription of a Terminal Sick Role." *Sociology and Social Research, LIII* (1969), 194–203.

Liton, J., and Olstein, S. C. "Therapeutic Aspects of Reminiscence." *Social Casework, L* (1969), 263–68.

Litwak, Eugene. "Geographical Mobility and Extended Family Cohesion." *American Sociological Review, XXV* (1960), 385–94.

————. "Occupational Mobility and Extended Family Cohesion." *American Sociological Review, XXV* (1960), 9–21.

Lopata, Helen Z. "The Social Involvement of American Widows." *American Behavioral Scientist, XIV* (September-October 1970), 41–47.

————. "Widows as a Minority Group." *The Gerontologist, XI* (Spring 1971), 67–77.

Lowenthal, Marjorie F. *Lives in Distress—Paths of the Elderly to the Psychiatric Ward*. New York: Basic Books, 1964.

Lowenthal, Milton, and others. "Nobody Wants the Incontinent." *R.N., XXI* (January 1958), 100–103.

Lowy, Louis. "The Group in Social Work with the Aged." *Social Work, VII* (October 1962), 43–50.

————. "Meeting the Needs of Older People on a Differential Basis." *Social Group Work with Older People*. New York: NASW, 1963.

Loyd, F. Glen, and Irwin, Theodore. "How Quackery Thrives on the Occult." *Today's Health*, November 1970, pp. 21–23, 87–88.

Maddison, David, and Raphael, Beverly. "The Family of the Dying Patient." New South Wales, Australia: University of Sydney, November 1970. (Mimeographed.)

Maddox, G. L. "Themes and Issues: Social Theories of Human Aging." *Human Development, XIII* (1970), 17–27.

Markson, Elizabeth. "The Geriatric House of Death: Hiding the Dying Elder in a Mental Hospital." *Aging and Human Development, I* (1970), 37–49.

Markson, Elizabeth Warren, and Hand, Jennifer. "Referral for Death: Low Status of the Aged and Referral for Psychiatric Hospitalization." Albany, N. Y.: Mental Health Research Unit, December 1969. (Mimeographed.)

Martin, Alexander Reid. *Leisure Time—A Creative Force*. Washington, D.C.: National Council on Aging, 1963.

Maslow, Abraham Harold. *Motivation and Personality*. Princeton, N. J.: Van Nostrand, 1954.

Maxwell, Jean M. *Centers for Older People*. New York: The National Council on the Aging, 1962.

May, Rollo. *Man's Search for Himself*. New York: New American Library, 1967.

McGandy, R. B., and others. "Nutrient Intake and Energy Expenditures in Men of Different Ages." *Journal of Gerontology, XXI* (1966), 581–87.

McKain, Walter C. *Retirement Marriage*. Storrs, Conn.: University of Connecticut, 1969.

McKinney, J. C., and De Vyver, F. T. *Aging and Social Policy*. New York: Appleton-Century-Crofts, 1966.

McTavish, Donald G. "Perceptions of Old People: A Review of Research Methodologies and Findings." *The Gerontologist, II* (Winter 1971), 90–101.

Mead, Margaret, Shepard, Elba W.; and Armiger, Sister Bernadette. "The Right to Die." *Nursing Outlook, XVI* (October 1968), 19–28.

Merril, S. E., and Funther, L. M. "A Study of Patient Attitudes Toward Older People." *Geriatrics, XXIV* (1969), 107–12.

Metchnikoff, E. *The Nature of Man: Studies in Optimistic Philosophy*. Translated by C. P. Mitchell. London: Heinemann, 1908.

Michal, Donald N. *The Unprepared Society, Planning or a Precarious Future*. New York: Harper and Row, 1970.

Miller, Michael B. "Challenges of the Chronically Ill Aged." *Geriatrics, XXV* (August 1970), 102–10.

Moore, Joan. "The Mexican-American." *The Gerontologist, II* (Spring 1971), 30–36.

————. "Situational Factors Affecting Minority Aging." *The Gerontologist, XI* (Spring 1971), 88–93.

Mutschler, Phyllis. "Factors Affecting Choice of and Perseveration in Social Work with the Aged." *The Gerontologist, II* (Fall 1971), 231–39.

Nash, B. E. "New Dimensions in Care of the Aging." *Hospital Process, LI* (1970), 69–72.

National Association of Social Workers. *Encyclopedia of Social Work.* 16th ed., 1971.

National Council on Aging. *Current Literature on Aging.* Washington, D.C.: NCOA, 1968–1972.

————. *Employment Prospects of Aged Blacks, Chicanos, and Indians.* Washington, D.C.: NCOA, 1971.

————. *The Golden Years: A Tarnished Myth.* New York: NCOA, 1970.

————. *Recommendations for Action in the Seventies.* Washington, D.C.: NCOA, 1971.

————. *Social Group Work with Older People.* New York: National Association of Social Workers, 1963.

National Institute of Mental Health. *Four Annotated Bibliographies on In-Service Training.* Washington, D.C.: The Institute, May 1969.

Neugarten, Bernice L., ed. *Middle Age and Aging.* Chicago, Ill.: University of Chicago Press 1968.

Neumeyer, Peter F. "What Is Relevant Literature." *The Record, CLXXI* (September 1969), 1–11.

Newfield, K. P. "Orientation to Later Maturity." *The Gerontologist, XI* (1971), 50.

Oberleder, Muriel. "An Attitude Scale to Determine Adjustment in Institutions for the Aged." *Journal of Chronic Disease, XV* (1961), 915–23.

————. "Emotional Breakdowns in Elderly People." *Hospital and Community Psychiatry, XX* (1969), 191–96.

————. "Psychological Characteristics of Older Age." Paper presented at the United States Department of Public Health Geriatric Training Conference, Philadelphia, Pa., September 1966. (Mimeographed.)

Orbach, Harold L., and others. *Trends in Early Retirement.* Ann Arbor, Mich.: University of Michigan, 1969.

Orshansky, Mollie. "The Aged Negro and His Income." *Social Security Bulletin.* Washington, D.C.: U. S. Department of Health, Education, and Welfare, 1964.

Palmore, Erdman. "Attitudes Toward Aging as Shown by Humor." *The Gerontologist, I* (Fall 1971), 181–87.

————, ed. *Normal Aging.* Durham, N. C.: Duke University Press, 1970.

Parad, Howard J. *Crisis Intervention: Selected Readings.* New York: Family Service Association of American, 1965.

Paterson, Josephine G. "From a Philosophy of Clinical Nursing to a Method of Nursology." *Nursing Research, XX* (March–April 1971), 143–46.

Pearl, R. *The Biology of Death.* Philadelphia: J. B. Lippincott, 1922.

Peters, Mary Overhold. "A Client Writes the Case Record." *The Family, XXVI* (November 1945), 258–61.

Pincus, Allen. "Reminiscence in Aging and Its Implications for Social Work Practice." *Social Work, XV* (July 1970), 47–53.

Post, Felix. "Dispelling the Gloom in Geriatric Psychiatry." *Geriatric Focus, VI* (May 1, 1967), 1.

Preston, Carolyn E. "Subjectively Perceived Agedness and Retirement." *Journal of Gerontology, XXIII* (April 1968), 201–205.

———, and others. "Views of the Aged on the Timing of Death." *The Gerontologist, XI* (Winter 1971), Chapter 13.

Rabinowitz, Dorothy, and Nielson, Yedida. *Home Life: A Story of Old Age.* New York: Macmillan, 1971.

Resnick, H. L. P., and Cantor, Joel M. "Suicide and Aging." *Journal of American Geriatrics Society, XVIII* (February 1970), 152–58.

Rice, Carolyn. "Old and Black." *Harvest Years, VIII* (November 1968), 38–45.

Rickles, Nathan K. "The Discarded Generation: The Woman Past Fifty." *Geriatrics, XXIII* (October 1968), 112–16.

Ridenour, Nina. *The Room Upstairs.* New York: American Association of Retired Persons, 1960.

Riesman, David. *Individualism Reconsidered.* Glencoe, Ill.: Free Press, 1954.

Riley, Matilda White, and others. *Aging and Society.* Vols. I and II. New York: Russell Sage Foundation, 1968 and 1970.

Rogers, Carl. *On Becoming a Person.* Boston: Houghton, Mifflin, 1961.

———, and Stevens, Barry, eds. *Person to Person: The Problem of Being Human.* New York: Simon and Schuster, 1971.

Rose, Arnold M., and Peterson, Warren A., eds. *Older People and Their Social World.* Philadelphia, Pa.: F. A. Davis, 1965.

Rose, Karel. "A Handbook of Selections About the Black Experience for Use in Teacher Education Courses for Prospective Elementary School Teachers." Unpublished Ed.D. dissertation, Teachers College, Columbia University, 1969.

Rosen, B. M.: Anderson, T. E.; and Bahn, A. K. "Psychiatric Services for the Aged: A Nationwide Survey of Patients of Utilization." *Journal of Chronic Diseases, XXI* (1968), 167–76.

Rosow, Irving. "Old Age: One Moral Dilemma of an Affluent Society." *The Gerontologist, II* (1962), 191.

———. *Social Integration of the Aged.* New York: Free Press, 1967.

Russell, Bertrand. "Your Child and the Fear of Death." *The Forum, LXXXI* (March 1929), 174–78.

Rybak, W. S.; Sadnavitch, J. M.; and Mason, B. J. "Psychosocial Changes in Personality During Foster Grandparents Program." *Journal of the American Geriatrics Society, XVI* (1968), 956–59.

Ryser, C., and Sheldon, A. "Retirement and Health." *Journal of the American Geriatrics Society, XVII* (1969), 180–90.

Saslow, George. "Summary: Opportunities and Obligations." *The Gerontologist, VIII* (Spring 1968), 57–58.

Saul, Shura. "Mental Illness in Aging." New York: Self-Help Community Services, 1970. (Mimeographed.)

———. "Teaching About Aging." *Council on Social Work Reporter, XX* (January 1972), 70–72.

———, and Boritzer, Rose. "An In-Service Program for Nurse's Aides." *Nursing Homes,* January 1969, p. 9.

Savitsky, Elias. "Psychological Factors in Nutrition of Aged." *Understanding the Older Client.* New York: Family Service Association of America, 1962.

———, and Starkman, Rosalind. *Teen Age Volunteer in a Home for the Aged.* New York: Psychiatric Department of the Kingbridge Home, Jewish Home and Hospital for the Aged, 1970.

Sheely, James H. *The Economic Status of the Retired Aged in 1980: Simulation Projections.* Washington, D.C.: U.S. Government Printing Office, 1968.

Scott, Colin A. "Old Age and Death." *American Journal of Psychology, VIII* (October 1968), 67–122.

Scott-Maxwell, Florida. *The Measure of My Days.* New York: Alfred A. Knopf, 1968.

Seltzer, Miriam M., and Atchley, Robert C. "The Concept of Old: Changing Attitudes and Stereotypes." *The Gerontologist, II* (Fall 1971), 226–31.

Selye, Hans. "Stress and Aging." *Journal of American Geriatric Society, XVIII* (September 1970), 669–80.

Shanas, Ethel. *The Health of Older People.* Cambridge, Mass.: Cambridge University Press, 1962.

———, ed. *The Multigeneration Family: Papers on Theory and Practice.* Trenton, N. J.: Department of State, Division on Aging, 1964.

———, and Streib, Gordon, eds. *Social Structure and The Family: Generational Relations.* Englewood Cliffs, N. J.: Prentice-Hall, 1965.

Shock, N. W., ed. *Biological Aspects of Aging.* 2nd ed. New York: Columbia University Press, 1962.

Simon, Alexander, and Epstein, Leon, eds. *Aging in Modern Society.* Washington, D.C.: American Psychiatric Association, February 1968.

Simon, Alexander; Lowenthal, Marjorie Fiske; and Epstein, Leon. *Crisis and Intervention. The Fate of the Elderly Mental Patient.* San Francisco, Calif.: Jossey-Bass, 1970.

Somers, Mary Louise. "Dimensions and Dynamics of Engaging the Learner." *Journal of Education for Social Work,* Fall 1971, pp. 49–59.

Somerville, Rose M. *Family Insights Through the Short Story.* New York: Bureau of Publication, Teachers College, Columbia University, 1964.

Soyer, David. "Reverie on Working with the Aged." *Social Casework, D* (1969), 291–94.

Spark, G. M., and Brody, E. M. "The Aged Are Family Members." *Family Process, IX* (1970), 195–210.

Spence, D. L., and others. "Medical Student Attitudes Toward the Geriatric Patient." *Journal of the American Geriatrics Society, XVI* (1968), 976–83.

Stein, Herman, and Cloward, Richard, eds. *Social Perspectives on Behavior.* Glencoe, Ill.: Free Press, 1959.

Stirling, Nora. *A Choice to Make.* New York: Family Service Association, 1963.

————. *Ever Since April.* New York: American Association of Retired Persons, 1960.

Stokes, Gertrude, ed., and others. *A Giant Step: The Roles of Psychiatric Nurses in Community Mental Health Practice.* New York: Maimonides Medical Center—Community Mental Health Center, 1969.

Stoller, F. H. "Accelerated Interaction: A Time-Limit Based on the Brief, Intensive Group." *International Journal of Group Psychotherapy, XVIII* (1968), 220–35.

Strehler, Bernard. "Ten Myths About Aging." Paper presented at University of Southern California Center Conference on Aging, September 1970. (Mimeographed.)

Streib, Gordon F. "Old Age in Ireland." *The Gerontologist, VIII* (1968), 227–35.

————. "Sociological Perspectives." *Journal of the American Geriatrics Society, XVII* (1969), 320–24.

Sussman, Marvin. "Family Continuity: Selective Factors Which Affect Relationships Between Families at Generational Levels." *Marriage and Family Living, XVI* (1954), 112–20.

Tallmer, Margot. "Disengagement and the Stresses of Aging." *Dissertation Abstracts, XXVIII* (1967), 2614–15.

————, and Kutner, Bernard. "Disengagement and the Stresses of Aging." *Journal of Gerontology, XXIV* (January 1969), 70–75.

Thompson, Prescott. "The Personal Physician, The Psychiatrist, The Family, and The Older Patient." *Journal of the American Geriatrics Society, XVI* (September 1968), 984–93.

————. "What It Means to Be Old Today." *Journal of the American Geriatrics Society, XIX* (April 1970), 337–40.

Tibbits, Clark. "Administration on Aging's Title V Training Grant Program." *The Gerontologist, X* (Spring 1970), 54–57.

————, ed. *Handbook of Social Gerontology*. Chicago: University of Chicago, 1960.

Tiven, Majorie Bloomberg. *Older Americans: Special Handling Required*. Washington, D.C.: National Council on Aging, 1971.

Towle, Charlotte. *Common Human Needs*. New York: National Association of Social Workers, 1957.

Townsend, Peter. *The Family Life of Old People*. London: Routledge and Kegan Paul, 1957.

Troll, Lillian, and Schlossberg, Nancy. "How Age Biased Are College Counselors?" *Industrial Gerontology*, Summer 1971, pp. 14–20.

Tuckman, Jacob, and Lorge, Irving. "Attitudes Towards Old People." *Journal of Social Psychology*, *XXXVII* (November 1953), 249.

————. "Attitudes Toward Aging of Individuals with Experiences with the Aged." *Journal of Genetic Psychology*, *XCII* (1958), 199–204.

Turner, Helen, ed. *Psychological Functioning of Older People*. Washington, D.C.: National Council on Aging, 1967.

Twente, Esther E. *Never Too Old, The Aged in Community Life*. San Francisco, Calif.: Jossey-Bass, 1970.

Ullman, Montague. "Powerlessness and the Elderly." New York: Maimonides Community Mental Health Center, 1970. (Mimeographed.)

U. S. Department of Health, Education, and Welfare. *Human Aging*. Edited by James E. Birren and others. Washington, D.C.: U. S. Government Printing Office, 1963.

————. *Words on Aging—Annotated Bibliography*. Washington, D.C.: U. S. Government Printing Office, October 1970.

————. *Working with Older People: A Guide to Practice*. 4 vols. Washington, D.C.: U. S. Government Printing Office, 1966, 1970, 1971.

U. S. Superintendent of Documents. *Mental Disorders of Aging*. Washington, D.C.: U.S. Government Printing Office, 1965.

————. *Nursing Care of the Aged*. Washington, D.C.: U. S. Government Printing Office, 1967.

————. *Our Elders*. Washington, D.C.: U. S. Government Printing Office, June 1968.

Vernick, Joel J. *Death and Dying. A Selected Bibliography*. Washington, D.C.: U. S. Government Printing Office, 1970.

Wagner, Ann, and Lerner, Joseph. "Art Therapy in a Psychiatric Hospital." *Journal of the American Geriatrics Society*, *XVI* (August 1968), 867–73.

Weaver, Charles N. "Influence of Sex, Salary, and Age on Seasonal Use of Sick Leave." *Personnel Journal*, August 1970, pp. 675–79.

Weinberg, Jack. "Environment, Its Language and the Aging." *Journal of American Geriatric Society*, *XVIII* (September 1970), 681–86.

Weiss, Curtis E. "Medicare and Communicative Therapy." *Journal of American Geriatric Society*, *XIX* (September 1971), 798–802.

Wheeler, Harvey. "The Rise of the Elders." *Saturday Review*, December 5, 1970, p. 14.

Williams, R. H., and Wirths, C. G. *Lives Through the Years: Styles of Life and Successful Aging.* New York: Atherton Press, 1965.

Wolff, Kurt. *The Emotional Rehabilitation of the Geriatric Patient.* Springfield, Ill.: Charles C. Thomas, 1970.

Wolk, Robert L., and Wolk, Rochelle B. "Professional Workers' Attitudes Towards the Aged." *Journal of the American Geriatrics Society, XIX* (1971), 624–39.

Woodrow, W. Morris. "Senile Psychosis Termed 'Cultural Artifact.' " *Geriatric Focus, VI,* May 15, 1968.

Wright, Irving S. "Geriatrics and the Challenges of the Seventies." *Journal of American Geriatric Society, XIX* (September 1971), 737–45.

Youmans, E. Grant. "Orientations to Old Age." *The Gerontologist VIII* (Autumn 1968), 153–58.

———. "Urban-Rural Comparison: Perceptions of Old Age." *The Gerontologist, II* (Winter 1971), 284–89.

Zemen, Frederick D. "Myths and Stereotypes in the Clinical Medicine of Old Age." *New England Journal of Medicine, CCLXXII* (May 27, 1965), 1104–1106.

Zinberg, N. E., and Glotfelty, J. A. "The Power of the Peer Group." *International Journal of Group Psychotherapy, XVIII* (1968), 155–64.

Zinberg, Norman E., and Kaufman, Irving. *Normal Psychology of the Aging Process.* New York: International Universities Press, 1963.